The Penguin Book
of Elementary Very Short Stories

The Penguin Book of Elementary Very Short Stories

Jake Allsop

PENGUIN
ENGLISH

PENGUIN ENGLISH

Published by the Penguin Group
Penguin Books Ltd, 27 Wrights Lane, London W8 5TZ, England
Penguin Books USA Inc., 375 Hudson Street, New York, New York 10014, USA
Penguin Books Australia Ltd, Ringwood, Victoria, Australia
Penguin Books Canada Ltd, 10 Alcorn Avenue, Toronto, Ontario, Canada M4V 3B2
Penguin Books (NZ) Ltd, 182–190 Wairau Road, Auckland 10, New Zealand

Penguin Books Ltd, Registered Offices: Harmondsworth, Middlesex, England

First published 1991
5 7 9 10 8 6

Copyright © Jake Allsop, 1991
All rights reserved

The moral right of the author has been asserted

Filmset in Monophoto Plantin
Printed in England by Clays Ltd, St Ives plc

Except in the United States of America,
this book is sold subject to the condition
that it shall not, by way of trade or otherwise,
be lent, re-sold, hired out, or otherwise circulated
without the publisher's prior consent in any form of
binding or cover other than that in which it is
published and without a similar condition
including this condition being imposed
on the subsequent purchaser

Contents

Introduction	1
All Those Noughts	3
Ladybirds	7
The Ninety-piece Man	12
This Bed is Cold	18
The Sorry Joke	21
A Postcard from Grandma	26
Out of the Way	30
Nice and Warm	35
Black Mud	39
The Orinoco Treasure	42
A Miracle on the Galata Bridge	48
Glossary and Language Practice	53

Introduction

As with my first collection, *The Penguin Book of Very Short Stories*, the stories in this book are very short. Each one is on average 1250 words long, so you should be able to read a story in one go.

You should not find the language difficult. The stories use a vocabulary of about 1700 headwords and most sentences are one or two clauses at the most.

At the back of the book, you will find a list of key vocabulary for each story. Unusual words or expressions are also explained. You will also find some language practice: comprehension, vocabulary exercises and a little bit of grammar (mainly phrasal verbs and prepositions). There is no key to these exercises because you can always find the answers by going back to the story. There are also some questions for discussion for students who are not working alone.

I hope you find the language practice useful and interesting, but, more than that, I hope you enjoy the stories. They are set in many different places – England, Israel, Italy, Switzerland, Tanzania and Turkey. They are about happy people and sad people, good people and bad people, funny people and frightening people, miracles and mysteries, love and jealousy, life and death.

Are they true stories? Well, the sixth story is exactly as it happened. As for the other stories, you must decide for yourself.

It is not usual to thank one's editor, but I want to thank

The Penguin Book of Elementary Very Short Stories

Michael Nation of Penguin Books. In the writing of this and my previous book of Very Short Stories, I would never have got very far without his help and good sense.

The book is dedicated to the memory of someone whom I loved very dearly. She enjoyed reading stories, and inspired me to write. Enjoy these stories as she would have done.

All Those Noughts

Sulo was a man that everybody noticed. He was a big man. He had the fat smooth face of a man who ate very well. He had a wonderful head of white hair. You knew he was someone important. And his clothes told you that he was a rich man. But he had not always been rich. He came from a poor family. He was Latvian or Estonian (nobody really knows: he had several passports which said he was Greek or Brazilian). He decided that he wanted to make money, and became very good at it. Before he was twenty, he had his own 'Import and Export' business in Rio, with branches in several other countries. He had two sayings. The first was: 'Buy cheap and sell dear'. The second was: 'Never look back'.

Yes, Sulo was rich – and dishonest. He often bought stolen goods at a low price and sold them at a high price. He used cash, never signed anything, and never paid taxes. As he left his Zurich hotel in a taxi to go to the airport, he patted the briefcase on his lap. What would people say, he thought, if they knew I had a million dollars in this briefcase! A million US dollars. He thought of their pretty green colour, of their pictures of the US Presidents and he thought of the number. All those noughts: US$1,000,000. Six beautiful noughts! Beautiful! He held the briefcase close to his body. Tonight, he thought, this money will be in a safe in Amsterdam. Sulo felt good.

Yanni was a man that nobody noticed. He was small and thin.

The Penguin Book of Elementary Very Short Stories

He did not look important. Nobody could ever remember his face. Yanni was Mr Nobody, always overlooked: he was invisible. He had Swiss identity documents, but he came from another country, Latvia or Estonia perhaps. He came from a poor family. When he was older, Yanni was glad that he was 'invisible', because it was useful for his work. His work? Yanni was a thief. And he was very good at it. Before he was twenty, he came to Zurich and got Swiss papers (nobody knows how). He became a specialist in picking pockets and stealing purses from handbags. He had only one saying: 'Little and often'.

He used to spend a lot of time at the main railway station, looking for 'customers'. Sometimes he liked to walk up Bahnhofstrasse and into one of the big department stores like Globus. Here it was easy to steal purses from open shopping bags. One day, his friend Dix, a specialist in stolen credit cards and foreign money, asked him:

'Yanni, have you ever thought of trying the Airport? There are lots of fat rich tourists there. Much better than the Railway Station, if you ask me.'

So, one day, Yanni took the bus out to the airport and went into Departures to see what he could find. At the KLM desk he noticed a big man with a fat face and a lovely head of white hair. He noticed that the man was having some trouble with the girl behind the counter. He noticed, too, that the man had put his briefcase on the ground. The man was too busy arguing with the girl to think about his case. It would be easy...

Sulo was angry.

'I booked the flight a week ago. I told your office in town that I would pick my ticket up at the airport today. So where is it?'

'I'm sorry, sir, but I have no record of the booking. Could you spell your name again?'

'Really! This is not good enough.'

He spelled out his name to her in the kind of loud slow voice that you use when talking to idiots:

All Those Noughts

'My name is Sulo. S-U-L-O. Now hurry up or I'll miss my flight to Amsterdam.'

After some more minutes, the girl finally found Sulo's booking; it was listed under Solo, an easy mistake to make. She gave Sulo his ticket.

'If you have only hand luggage, sir, you can go straight through now.'

'Good. Yes,' Sulo said, 'I only have my br . . .'

He looked down. The briefcase had disappeared. He looked round, his eyes wild. For a moment he thought he was going to faint. His face was white. It wasn't possible! It just wasn't possible! He stared at the place where he had put the case down, as if he expected it to reappear. Suddenly, he felt as if he was going to be sick. He had to go to the toilet. Quickly.

While Sulo was arguing at the KLM desk Yanni went downstairs to the toilet. He went into the nearest cubicle and closed the door behind him. He was quite excited. A briefcase could contain all sorts of useful things: a calculator perhaps, or some expensive pens. Or some foreign money. Dix would buy that from him. Or there would be some credit cards. Dix would be happy to take them too.

'Little and often,' he said to himself, smiling. 'Steal a little, steal often.' He began to sing softly, because Yanni was happy in his work, unlike most people.

He sat on the toilet, put the briefcase on his knees, rubbed his hands and opened the case. He cried out when he saw the piles of green banknotes. Millions and millions of US dollars! He felt afraid. His face went white and he felt sick. Big money like this was big trouble, and he didn't want any trouble.

'What shall I do? What shall I do?'

He wished that Dix was there to help him. Dix would know what to do.

'Perhaps I should put it down the toilet,' he thought. 'No, that would take a long time. No. Just leave it! Leave it and get out, fast!'

He felt angry now. He hated the big man with the fat face

and the white hair. Why couldn't he just carry a few credit cards and a *small* quantity of cash like normal people? Why didn't he have something that an honest thief could steal. Not millions and millions of dollars like this. This was stupid. Too much money. No good for anybody. Yanni closed the case and hit the lid with his fists.

'It's just not fair!' he said out loud. He put the briefcase out of sight behind the toilet. He hoped that nobody would find it before he had got away from the airport.

'Let's get back to Bahnhofstrasse and steal a few purses, purses that have *normal* amounts of money in them. A few francs here, a few francs there . . .'

As he went up the stairs, he saw the big man with the white hair coming down. Yanni's heart stopped. He looked away quickly. Sulo did not even notice him.

Sulo went downstairs and ran into the nearest cubicle. He closed the door and sat on the toilet, his head in his hands.

'How could I have been so stupid?' he asked himself. 'A million dollars! A million dollars! And some dirty little thief has stolen it! Well, if I ever catch him, I'll kill him. There are thieves everywhere nowadays. The world isn't safe for decent people any more.'

It was good to get angry. It made him feel better. But not much better. He realized that there was nothing he could do about the lost money. He got up and went out of the cubicle. The briefcase was still behind the toilet, but Sulo did not look back. Sulo never looked back.

Ladybirds

[A ladybird is a garden beetle. It is red with black spots. Ladybirds are pretty and everybody likes them.]

'What are you doing?'

The old man looked up to see who had asked the question. He saw a little girl standing near him.

'That is a very good question,' he said. 'You mean, why am I down here on my hands and knees?'

She nodded.

'Yes, a very good question,' he repeated. 'What do *you* think I am doing?'

She frowned. He was just like a teacher. He always answered a question with a question.

'Are you looking for something? Have you lost something?'

'No, my dear, I haven't lost anything. So, what do you think I am looking for here in the long grass?'

'I don't know. Please tell me.'

'First, tell me your name.'

'Rebecca. What's yours?'

He decided that he liked this little girl. She was not shy or silly.

'Well, Rebecca, you can call me Poff. Everybody does.'

'Poff.' She paused. 'Poff,' she said again. 'That's a funny name. Is it your real name?'

'Another very good question, Rebecca. You're full of good questions. You want to know what I am looking for in the long grass. Let me show you. Look at this.'

He took a box from his pocket and opened it. She looked inside. It was full of small pieces of newspaper.

'Is that all?' she said. 'Just old bits of paper?'

'No, my dear. Look again.'

He put his finger into the box and moved the bits of paper round. She could see then that there were a lot of shiny black insects in the box. 'Do you like them, Rebecca?'

She looked into the box again.

'They're very pretty. May I pick one up?'

The old man smiled. He was very pleased. She was not afraid of insects. She did not scream or run away. She was interested in insects.

'Of course, but be very careful. Here, hold your hand out.'

He picked up one of the insects and put it into her hand. She studied it, her face very serious. The insect ran across her hand, and dropped into the grass.

'Oh I'm sorry!' she said, afraid that the man would be angry with her.

'Don't worry, Rebecca. I have a lot more in the box.'

'Why are you collecting these ... black things?'

'They're insects, Rebecca, and I want to study them.'

'Why?'

The old man scratched his head. How could he explain to this small child? She would not understand words like 'study' or 'science'.

'Because they are interesting.'

'Interesting?' It was a new word for Rebecca. She liked new words.

'Yes. Interesting. You see, I want to know as much about their lives as I can.'

'Why?' she asked.

'Come, let me show you some other insects that I have collected.'

She looked into the box again. She moved the bits of paper with her finger and found several different kinds of insects:

Ladybirds

yellow and gold and brown and red. Her hair touched the old man's cheek. He looked at her and felt lonely.

'They *are* very ... interesting,' she said, enjoying the new word. 'Can I help you to find some more? Where do they live? In the grass?'

She went down on her hands and knees next to him. Soon they were busy looking for more insects to add to his collection. The old man felt happy. It was nice to have a friend. It was nice to be with someone who was as interested in insects as he was.

'Look at this one!' he said, holding up a large black beetle with long horns.

Rebecca clapped her hands.

'That's the biggest one of all!' she said. 'Can I have it? Please, Poff, can I keep it?'

'Well, Rebecca, I don't think your mummy would be very happy if you took a big black beetle into the house. Especially one with horns.'

She thought about this for a time.

'Yes, Poff,' she said in a serious voice, 'I think you're right. Mummy gets angry about so many things.'

'Let's put it in the box with the others,' he said softly. She looked sad.

'Come on,' he said, 'see if you can find me some ladybirds.'

'Which ones are ladybirds?'

'The pretty red ones with black spots on. When you find one, count the spots.'

'How many spots do they have, Poff? Do they have lots and lots of spots?'

'Well, you count them and then you will see.'

Poff thought of the scientific name, *Coccinella 7-punctata*. Let her find the seven spots for herself. It was the best way for her to learn and remember. Rebecca was already on her hands and knees. The grass was so long that she almost disappeared. Poff could just see her fair hair above the grass.

The Penguin Book of Elementary Very Short Stories

'Got one!' she shouted. She stood up and held out her hand. 'I've got one, Poff! A really pretty one!'

He loved her for loving beetles as much as he did.

'Well done, Rebecca! Now, count the spots.'

He waited, remembering the first time he had counted the seven spots on a ladybird.

'Five!' she shouted. 'There are five spots, aren't there, Poff? Is that right?'

'No, dear, not quite right. Look again. There are three on each wing. That makes six. And there's another spot on the neck, just behind the head. That makes seven. Can you find them all?'

She looked again at her prize. Very closely. He watched as she counted the spots out loud: one, two ... three, four ... five. She shook her head, and counted again. But she could only see five. She felt stupid. Poff would think that she was very stupid. She didn't know what to say.

'Can't you find the other two?' he said, coming over to her. Perhaps the poor child cannot count, he thought to himself. He knelt down next to her. She held her hand out to him to show him the ladybird. He took her hand in his and looked at the beetle.

'Let me see.'

She was right! It was amazing! The central wing spots were missing. There were indeed only five spots. Poff had never seen a five-spot ladybird before. Was it a new kind, *Coccinella 5-punctata*? Or was it just a strange ladybird? It didn't matter: this was an exciting thing to find, and Poff was excited! I'll take it to the Museum, he thought. I'll show it to my friend, Dr Booth. I'll be famous. I'll be 'Poff, the man who found the first five-spot ladybird'!

'You're right, Rebecca! You're right! Only five spots! It's wonderful! What a clever girl you are. Thank you! Thank you!'

He picked her up and lifted her above his head, laughing. Rebecca laughed too. She was happy because Poff was happy.

She was happy because he did not think she was stupid for finding only five spots. Poff was soon out of breath. He put her down and patted her head.

'Can I keep it, Poff? Please. I promise to look after it, and I'm sure mummy wouldn't mind if I took a ladybird into the house.'

He held her hand again and they looked together at the ladybird. How could he tell her that he needed this insect? She could have all the others, but not this one. Suddenly, a woman's voice, a loud angry voice, made them jump.

'So there you are, Rebecca! I've been looking everywhere for you! Come home at once. At once, do you hear!'

'As for you, old man,' Rebecca's mother said, looking at Poff angrily, 'you should be ashamed!'

Poff's cheeks burned red. He let go of Rebecca's hand, but he made sure she was still holding the five-spot ladybird. 'It is a very special ladybird, Rebecca,' he whispered. 'Look after it well.' Then he turned and walked quickly away.

The Ninety-piece Man

[In Italy, an important person is sometimes called a *pezzo novanta*. *Pezzo* means 'piece' and *novanta* means 'ninety'.]

Sue stared at the white van. Then she turned to her husband.
'What is *that*?' she asked.
'It's a Volkswagen camper. It's got a cooker, beds, everything. We can go to Italy in it this summer.'
'James, you can't be serious!'
'Of course I'm serious. Katy will get you and me and the children to Italy. No problem. She's a wonderful old van.'
'Katy?'
James pointed to the number plate: KT 343.
'K – T. Kay – tee. Katy.'
'Very nice. But I don't want to travel across Europe in it. What happens if it breaks down? There we'll be: on an Italian motorway . . .'
'*Autostrada.*'
'What?'
'*Autostrada.* That's Italian for "motorway".'
'On an Italian motorway,' said Sue, ignoring him, 'in the middle of nowhere, the children tired and thirsty, and nobody who speaks English.'
'Don't worry, Sue. Katy won't break down. She's a good van.'
'"She?" Don't you mean "it"?' said Sue. James said nothing. He patted Katy's side.

The Ninety-piece Man

'Oh, all right,' said Sue. 'We'll go to Italy in your van. But I refuse to call it "Katy". It's just a van. And it's certainly not female. OK?'

'Italy, here we come!' he shouted.

The Italian sun was hot. The children were tired and thirsty. Sue was tired and thirsty and angry. James was under the van, trying to find out what was wrong. On the *autostrada*, cars and lorries and vans went past at high speed. This is not pleasant to watch when your own van has broken down.

James stood up. His hands and face were black.

He started to explain what was wrong. 'I think there's a broken blah blah blah blah . . .'

To Sue, it was a foreign language.

'I have no idea what you're talking about. Just tell me one thing: can you mend it?'

James looked at Sue. He looked at his hands. He looked at the sky. Then he looked at Sue again.

'Hm. Well, I . . . That is to say . . . Hm, well, it's not easy . . . If only I had . . .'

'In others words, no.'

James looked at his hands and at the sky again. Then he looked at Sue. It was time to tell the truth.

'Yes. Right. The answer is no, I cannot mend it.'

That was the truth. James felt better. He sat down on the grass, lay back and closed his eyes.

'You're not going to sleep, are you? James! What are we going to do? We can't stay here. It will be dark soon.'

'I am thinking.'

'It's a pity you didn't think before you bought this . . . this . . . thing.'

'Don't be unkind. Katy is not a thing. She is a good old van, but, like all old things, she has a few problems sometimes.'

'Well, Mr Carson, your "good old van" has broken down. It won't go. This van is sick. If it was a horse, you would shoot it. And the driver. Right now, if I had a gun, I'd . . .'

Before Sue could tell her husband that she was ready to shoot him a car stopped behind them. There were two men in the car: the driver and an older man sitting in the back. The driver got out and came up to them.

65 *'Buona sera, signori! Posso aiutarvi?'*

Sue smiled at him. When she spoke to him, she spoke very loudly. He will understand English if I shout, she thought.

'THANK YOU! I'M AFRAID WE DON'T SPEAK ITALIAN!! WE HAVE BROKEN DOWN!! MY HUS-
70 BAND DOES NOT KNOW WHAT TO DO!!'

The young man smiled. He did not understand a word.

'Scusi, signora, non capisco.'

Sue decided to try another method: baby talk.

'ME NO UNDERSTAND ITALIAN! THIS CAR NO
75 GOOD! NO GO! VERY BAD! YOU HELP? YES? *SI? PER FAVORE?*'

'That's really very good, Sue!' said James. 'You didn't tell me that you could speak Italian!'

'All right, you try to explain to him what's wrong. Tell him
80 about the broken thing . . .'

'Thing? Oh, you mean the broken blah blah blah . . .'

James explained the problem for the second time, and Sue understood nothing for the second time.

'Look, Mr James Clever Carson,' she screamed, 'I know you
85 can't speak Italian. It's a pity you can't speak English either!'

She lifted her hands in the air and looked up at the sky.

'I HATE vans and I HATE men!'

She felt better after that.

The driver was listening carefully. He didn't understand,
90 but he smiled anyway. He liked English people. They are always so calm in a crisis.

The older man got out of the car.

'Cosa c'è? What's the matter?'

The driver explained about the language problem.

95 'Good afternoon,' said the older man in perfect English.

The Ninety-piece Man

'May I introduce myself? My name is Donzelli. Signore Enzo Donzelli. At your service. My card.'

He handed his card to James but Sue took it. The card was clean and white with gold lettering. It said that he was Dott. Enzo Donzelli of Rome, Director of The Donzelli Import–Export Company. It also showed that he had offices in Milan, Turin and Naples, and a lot of telephone lines, telexes and fax numbers.

She thanked him, pointed at the van, shook her head, and said:

'It won't go.'

Signor Donzelli looked at the old VW camper.

'Ah yes, the Volkswagen. A wonderful German machine. But at the moment it is not wonderful, because it will not go. Well, don't worry, *cara Signora*. I shall send a mechanic to see to it. *Arrivederci*.'

'How kind of Mr Donzelli to help us like that,' Sue said.

They were speeding down the autostrada in Katy. James did not reply.

'Why did the mechanic refuse to take any money? Wasn't that kind of him? Italians are very kind, aren't they?'

'I could have mended the van myself,' James said.

'Really, dearest? So why did you say earlier that you couldn't mend it?'

'I never said that!'

'Yes you did!'

'No I didn't!'

'Yes you did!'

'No I didn't!'

The children were enjoying the scene. They loved it when mum and dad argued.

'Yes you did, daddy!' said one of them.

'Be quiet, children!' said Sue. 'Don't upset your father.'

James smiled.

130 'Anyway,' he said, 'Katy is going well now. I told you there was nothing to worry about!'

The children were hot and thirsty. They were sitting on the grass by the side of the road. Sue was standing by the van, her face as black as thunder. James was under the van. He looked 135 up at Sue.

'Another broken blah blah blah?'

'Yes.'

'Can you . . .?'

'No.'

140 'Good! Wonderful! What an exciting holiday! Have you any more surprises for us? An earthquake? A revolution? World War Three, perhaps?'

'I'll hitchhike to the nearest town and get a mechanic.'

Several hours later, a smiling mechanic patted the van.

145 'She is good. She will go now. No problem.'

He wrote something on a piece of paper and gave it to James.

'*Il conto*. The bill, if you please.'

James looked at the number at the bottom of the bill. It 150 started with 99 and had a lot of noughts after it. James changed the number into pounds. There were not so many noughts, of course, but it was still a lot. James knew that he did not have enough money to pay the bill.

'This is too much!' James said.

155 The mechanic shrugged and smiled.

'*Mi dispiace, ma* . . . I'm sorry, but that is the price for such a repair.'

James looked at the bill again. He looked at Sue. He looked at the sky. He looked at his hands and then at the grass on 160 which the children were sitting. He made a decision. He gave the bill to Sue and said to her:

'Tell him that we cannot pay.'

Then he sat down on the grass, lay back and closed his eyes. The mechanic did not understand. He did not know that the

The Ninety-piece Man

English always remain calm in a crisis. He turned to Sue and began to shout at her in Italian.

Sue knew that she needed a miracle now. She remembered Donzelli's white card with the gold lettering. She showed it to the mechanic.

'Please telephone Mr Donzelli and explain the situation. He is a friend of ours. He will help us.'

The mechanic looked at the card. His mouth fell open. He handed the card back to Sue. Then he took the bill from her, and said:

'No problem. My mistake. You owe me nothing. Please, you owe me nothing. *Arrivederci!*'

'Excuse me,' said Sue, 'but who *is* Signor Donzelli? Do you know him?'

'*Si signora*. Everyone knows him. He is a real *pezzo novanta*.'

'A what?'

But the mechanic had already left. James opened his eyes.

'Well done, old girl! By the way, what did he say about Donzelli?'

'I'm not sure. I *think* he said that Mr Donzelli was a ninety-piece man.'

'The Italians are strange, aren't they? Strange, but very kind. Come on, Sue, let's go. Katy will get us home.'

'I'm sure she will,' said Sue, 'thanks to my friend the ninety-piece man.'

This Bed is Cold

This bed is cold. It's the middle of summer, the sun is shining, and I am cold. Well, I don't care. I told him to leave, and he left. It seems days ago, but he walked out only a few hours ago. Let him go to that other woman. I don't care. He will soon find out that I am a better woman than she is. She is horrible. Everyone knows that. She loves to steal other women's husbands. I saw the way he looked at her the other night at the party. Stupid. He's stupid. Typical man! He runs after every woman who smiles at him. He's like a little dog.

How did the quarrel start? Well, *I* didn't start it. I'm not the jealous type. *He* started it. He came home late again last night. I wasn't jealous, I just wanted to know where he had been.

'*Oh, I met Bill Brown, and we went for a drink.*'

Bill Brown! Does Bill Brown wear perfume? I can smell perfume on you, you liar. A woman's perfume. Her perfume.

'*Really? I thought Bill Brown was in the States on business.*'

Be casual, don't get angry. Don't let him see that you know.

'*He was in the States. He got back yesterday.*'

Oh, how easily you lie! Do you think I am a fool? Do you think I don't know where you have been? Do you think I don't know who you have been with?

'*Where did you go for a drink?*'

'*Why are you asking so many questions, darling? Is something wrong?*'

This Bed is Cold

How can you call me 'Darling'? You have just been in the arms of another woman? I can smell her! You ... you ...

'No, nothing's wrong. I'm interested, that's all. It doesn't matter.'

Walk out of the room. Go into the kitchen. Get away from him.

Why am I so cold? Why is this bed so cold on a hot day like this? He followed me into the kitchen. He put his arms round me. He kissed the back of my neck. I used to love that, but not any more. He's been with another woman. A woman knows these things. And he thinks he is so clever. Men are little boys. They think they can hide the truth, but they can't. He kissed the back of my neck in that wonderful way he has. But I didn't move. I hate him now.

'What's wrong, darling? Are you sure you're all right?'

I didn't answer him. I pushed him away, and told him to leave me alone. He looked shocked. No, not shocked. He looked guilty, like a little boy who has been naughty. I had found out the truth, and he knew it. Good! He has made me suffer. Now he can suffer.

I went to bed soon after that. I didn't want to talk to him. I didn't want to look at him. When he came to bed he put his hand on my shoulder. But I did not want to feel his hands on me. Those hands had touched another woman only hours before. Well, if she's so wonderful, he can go back to her. What does he see in her? She's much older than me and she has bad skin. She uses too much makeup. And she's fat. How can he prefer her to me? It's horrible.

'Please don't touch me!'

He has beautiful hands. They are strong but gentle. How could he touch another woman with those strong, beautiful hands?

'What is the matter, darling? Have I done something wrong? Please tell me.'

Ignore him. Say nothing. Make him suffer.

'Look, I'm sorry I was late. But I hadn't seen Bill for such a long time ...'

'Bill Brown! Don't lie to me! I know who you were with. Why don't you go back to her now?'

'Her? Who? What are you talking about? Oh, no! Not again! I've told you a thousand times. You do not need to be jealous. I love you. Other women don't interest me.'

I hate his lies. His voice is always so smooth when he lies. I decided not to say another word to him. He told me again that he loved me. He said that I was the only woman for him. It was all rubbish.

Finally, he was silent. He got up and went downstairs. When he came back he spoke angrily. But I was strong. I said nothing. Let him suffer.

He ran downstairs. I heard the front door close.

Men! They're all the same. I suppose he's gone to his mother's. That's what men usually do when life gets too difficult for them. They run to mummy like little boys. He had kissed the back of my neck, hoping that all his problems would go away. But it didn't work. Now he's running back to mummy.

What's that? The front door! He's come back! I knew he would. They always come back. Calm now. Don't be too soft. I don't want him to think that he has won. I should brush my hair. No! Why should I? Let him take me as I am. He's coming up here. Well, he can speak first. He must make the peace.

He's gone again. He just walked into the bedroom, packed his suitcase and walked out again without saying a word. He didn't even look at me. But he'll come back. He always comes back. He has always come back the other times. I love him. He knows that.

This bed is cold. It's the middle of summer, the sun is shining, and I am cold. Yes, he'll come back. They always do. Men.

The Sorry Joke

'Good morning, sir! You are British, sir? Yes? *Karibu!* Welcome, sir! Welcome to my town. God save the Queen!'

Tor turned round and saw an old African behind him. The man was very thin. He wore a jacket that was too big for him, and a pair of old, torn trousers. His hat was made of leather, and was even older than his trousers. He had staring eyes and looked mad.

'Er, good morning,' Tor replied. 'No, I am not British. As a matter of fact I'm Swedish.'

'Good!' replied the old African. '*Karibu!* Welcome. I have met many British people. They are good people. Are you from London?'

'No. I'm not British. I'm from Stockholm,' said Tor. 'That's in Sweden,' he added.

'I am Professor Samahani Kejeri,' said the man. He waited. Tor smiled, said nothing, and got back into his van. The Professor put his head through the window.

'Samahani – that means "sorry" in my language. Kejeri – that means "joke". So, you see, I am Professor Sorry Joke.' He smiled, but only with his mouth: his eyes remained cold. Tor nodded.

'*Karibu*, sir. Welcome. Do you want to see the Kaole Ruins? Everyone wants to see the Kaole Ruins. Come, we shall go to the Kaole Ruins. You will see where the Arabs lived and where they took the slaves. Come, Kejeri will show you all these terrible things.'

The Penguin Book of Elementary Very Short Stories

He did not wait for an answer. He climbed into the van. It was hopeless. There was no escape from this madman. Kejeri pointed straight ahead. Tor started the engine and set off in the direction of Kejeri's pointing finger.

'Do you know Professor Roy Williams of London University? Of course. Well, he and I were the first to find the Kaole Ruins.'

'Oh, when was that?' Tor asked.

Kejeri looked away.

'Professor Williams and I were digging at Kaole for many years,' he said. 'And at last we found the ruins of the city built by the Arab slave traders. You will see.'

'Is Professor Williams still here?' asked Tor.

'No.'

'What happened to him?'

'He left.'

'When?'

Kejeri seemed unwilling to answer.

'When did he leave?' Tor asked again.

'After Independence, sir. Everyone left. Now Kejeri is in charge. You will see.'

Tor liked the way the old African said 'Kejeri', as if he was talking about someone else. It was a wonderful name. It sounded like an African drumbeat: sam-a-*HAN*-i ke-*JER*-i. What a pity its English translation was 'Sorry Joke'. If that is true, thought Tor.

When they arrived at the old Arab town Kejeri led Tor to a small hut. It was made of sticks and banana leaves. It would fall down if you sneezed near it, Tor thought. It had a big locked door made of heavy wood. Kejeri took out a rusty key. As he did so, Tor noticed that he had a huge knife hanging from his belt. Kejeri unlocked the door and told Tor to go inside.

'*Karibu!* You are welcome. Please sit down.'

Tor did not feel at all comfortable. He was alone in a dark hut with a man who was no professor, a man with cold eyes, a man who carried a terrible knife . . .

The Sorry Joke

'Look at this, sir. You see, many British people like yourself have visited Kejeri's Office at Kaole.'

Office! This little hut! Tor was glad that the old man could not see his face in the darkness. The old man was holding out a book. Tor tried to forget the knife. He took the book that Kejeri was offering to him. It was a desk diary for the year 1964. Wasn't that the year when Tanganyika became independent?

'Read it, please. You will see.'

There were dozens of scraps of paper on every page, and postcards, letters and business cards. Tor got up and went to the door so that he could see them better. They came from people from all over the world: from Britain, Germany, France, Italy, the USA, Japan, Brazil ... He read some of the messages: 'Thank you, Professor Kejeri, for a wonderful day at Kaole'. 'Professor Kejeri, you are doing a wonderful job'. 'I was amazed at your knowledge of Kaole'. 'Thank you, Professor Kejeri, we will come back one day'.

The old African was watching Tor's face closely.

'You see how many British people know Kejeri! Perhaps you will meet them when you go back to London. Tell them that Kejeri remembers them.'

'I'm not Brit ...' Tor did not finish the sentence. As far as Kejeri was concerned, all white men were British.

'Yes, of course,' he said, 'when I am back in London I will tell them what you say.'

Kejeri did not say thank you but he smiled again.

'Now, let us go to see the Kaole Ruins,' he said.

Kejeri pointed out the streets and the black-bricked walls of houses and shops. He showed Tor the 'harem' or women's quarters of a rich man's house. There was a cemetery, too, where people were buried. One or two stones still had Arab writing on them.

'See the writing,' said Kejeri. He went over to one of the stones. 'This one says FATIMA. That is a woman's name in Arabic.'

He was proud of his knowledge. He ran his finger over the Arab letters. Tor smiled when he noticed that Kejeri's finger moved from left to right over the letters. 'Professor' Kejeri does not know everything, thought Tor.

'And there is the mosque, the holy church of the Muslims.'

Kejeri was pointing to a tower. It was not the minaret of a mosque, but the remains of a chimney. Tor was sure now that Kejeri was not a professor. He must have worked at the site for Williams as a labourer. But this simple man, with torn clothes and his terrible knife hanging from his belt, was now the expert on Kaole. Tor remembered an old proverb: 'In the country of the blind, the one-eyed man is king.'

They walked to a very big building where the traders used to keep the slaves. Next to it were some smaller buildings. Kejeri told Tor that they were the 'Baluchi barracks'.

'Baluchi barracks?'

'Yes, sir. The Arabs brought soldiers from Baluchistan. This is where the Baluchi soldiers lived. Bad men, sir. Cruel men. Many slaves came here. Many slaves died.'

These slaves were Africans, his own people, people like Kejeri, thought Tor. What does he think about this place and these events? Does he ever think of revenge? The knife that he carries...

It was a fascinating place, but it was a terrible place. Tor shivered when he remembered Kejeri's terrible knife. It was time to leave the Kaole Ruins.

They drove back, past the village where the Baluchis still lived, past the old prison where the slaves were held. Suddenly Kejeri signalled to Tor to stop.

'Look there, sir.'

He was pointing to a tree with overhanging branches.

'That is the "Hanging Tree", sir. In colonial times prisoners were hanged there, in front of all the people.'

'Public hangings?'

'Yes, sir. It was a warning. In colonial times the people in charge said: "We are the masters here. You must obey our laws."'

The Sorry Joke

Tor did not know what to say.

'There were many laws, sir. Many prisoners. Many hangings in those days. See where the rope has cut into the branch.'

The two men were standing by the van. Tor was feeling very uncomfortable. His mouth was dry. He had seen and heard too much. He wanted to get into his van and drive away. Quickly.

He looked at Kejeri. It seemed to Tor that the old African was waiting for something. But for what? Words? Tor cleared his throat.

'Ahem. Thank you very much K . . .' – no, thought Tor, he deserves his title – 'Thank you very much, Professor Kejeri. I have seen a lot of interesting things.'

Still the old man seemed to wait. Tor thought again. Ah, yes! He remembered the little hut and the book which the old man had proudly shown him.

'Here is my card to add to your . . . to your collection. And I shall certainly tell everyone in . . . er, London . . . that I have met you.'

Kejeri took the card and put it in his pocket with the rusty key, next to the long knife. He did not smile or say thank you. And still he seemed to be waiting for something.

Money! thought Tor suddenly. Perhaps he expects a tip! Perhaps he is just like guides everywhere. He wants to be paid. But how much money do you give a man like Kejeri? If you give him too much, he will think you are a fool; if you give him too little, you will insult him. And what if I am wrong? He is a very proud man. He will become angry. He has a knife . . .

Tor jumped into his van and drove away. No goodbyes. No handshakes. No tips. Nothing. Tor looked in his driving mirror. The old African had not moved. His face remained unsmiling, his eyes staring.

Tor felt terrible. He heard again the old man's voice as he announced his drumbeat name: I am Sam-a-*HAN*-i Ke-*JER*-i.

And a question formed in Tor's mind: 'Which of us is the "Sorry Joke" now?'

A Postcard from Grandma

[This is a true story except for the names. Nobody has been able to explain the mystery. Perhaps you can explain it.]

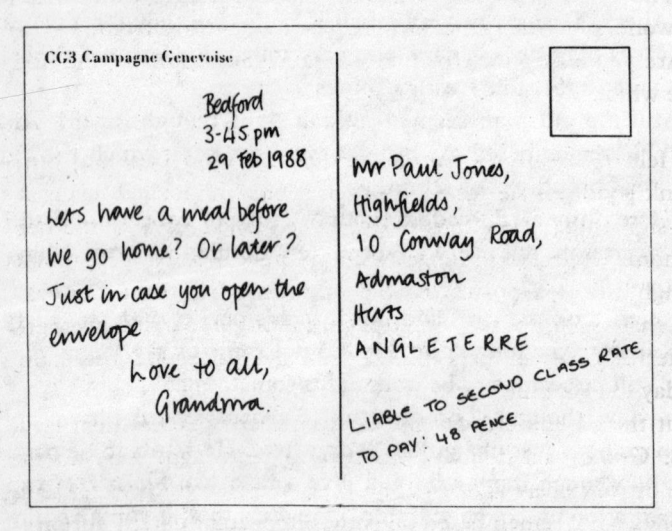

> CG3 Campagne Genevoise
>
> Bedford
> 3·45 pm
> 29 Feb 1988
>
> Lets have a meal before we go home? Or later? Just in case you open the envelope
>
> Love to all,
> Grandma.
>
> Mr Paul Jones,
> Highfields,
> 10 Conway Road,
> Admaston
> Herts
> ANGLETERRE
>
> LIABLE TO SECOND CLASS RATE
> TO PAY: 48 PENCE

One morning in early March the postman knocked on the door of the Joneses' house in Admaston.

'Good morning, Mrs Jones. Lovely day.'

15 'Yes, isn't it?'

Janet Jones waited, wondering why he had knocked on the door. Usually, he only did that when he had something that was too big to go through the letterbox. But all he had in his hand was a postcard.

20 'I'm afraid the postcard hasn't got a stamp on it. There's 48 pence to pay.'

A Postcard from Grandma

'Oh sorry,' said Mrs Jones, as if it were her fault there was no stamp on the postcard. 'Just a moment.' She went into the house and came back with the money.

'It's strange how people sometimes to forget to put stamps on,' said the postman. 'Of course you have had to pay more because the postcard is from abroad.'

Janet looked at the postcard. It was a picture postcard of trees and fields with the words 'Campagne Genevoise' – the Geneva countryside – on it.

'Who on earth would send us a postcard from Switzerland?' she wondered. She turned it over to see who it was from.

'Are you all right, Mrs Jones?' asked the postman. She had gone white.

She felt better after a cup of tea. Her husband Paul was out. Thank goodness he would be back soon. She looked again at the signature: 'Grandma'. Everyone called Paul's mother 'grandma', ever since the grandchildren were little. OK, that's all right. It is a postcard from grandma. It's from Geneva. OK, that's all right too, because grandma's unmarried brother, Frederick, worked in Geneva, and she had gone there on holiday to visit him.

But the dates were wrong. The postmark said 29 February 1988. Grandma's holiday was several years ago. Yes, about three or four years ago. In 1984. Yes, she went to Switzerland in 1984. Janet remembered one other important date: February 1986, when grandma died.

Paul sat at the kitchen table, staring at the postcard. He could not believe it. Janet felt better now that he was here. She made him a cup of tea and sat down next to him.

'It must be a joke,' she said, 'A very cruel joke. Who would do such a terrible thing?'

Paul shook his head.

'No, love, it isn't a joke. This is my mother's handwriting. This postcard was written by her. I am sure of that.'

'Perhaps she left it in a drawer in the hotel, and someone found it and posted it.'

'I don't think she stayed in a hotel. She stayed with Frederick, didn't she?'

'Perhaps Frederick found it and . . .'

She stopped. Of course, Frederick was also dead now.

'Read the message again,' she said.

'Let's have a meal before we go home? Or later?'

'"We?" Who does she mean? And "go home" to where?'

Paul shook his head. 'I don't know. Perhaps she wanted to come here for a meal before she went back to her home in London. What about the next sentence: *"Just in case you open the envelope"*. What envelope does she mean?'

'Perhaps she put this postcard in an envelope,' Janet said.

'Yes?'

'Well, perhaps she put the postcard in an envelope and forgot to post it and someone found it and opened the envelope and . . . Oh, I don't know? It just doesn't make sense!'

She was beginning to get upset again. Paul patted her on the arm.

'Now, now, love, don't get upset. There must be an explanation.'

'All right, but explain to me why it was posted in Bedford. Who do we know in Bedford? Nobody.'

Paul frowned. It seemed that everything about the postcard from Grandma was a mystery. But the biggest mystery was still to come.

The same evening Paul spent a long time looking at the postcard. He took out a piece of paper and wrote down every word that was on the postcard, printed or written. He looked at his old diaries, he read old letters from members of his family. He even telephoned several people who might have useful information. Finally, he took out a clean sheet of paper and made a short list. Then he turned to Janet.

'Janet,' he said, 'do you remember grandma's "twenty-first" birthday party?'

A Postcard from Grandma

His wife smiled. It was a family joke that grandma was only twenty-one years old in 1980.

'Oh yes!' she said. 'That was a wonderful day. She really enjoyed herself. It was lovely to see her with all her grandchildren round her.'

'When was that exactly?' asked Paul. He sounded like a detective in a novel.

'February 1980, of course.'

'Exactly. February the twenty-ninth.'

He paused for a moment and then asked another question.

'And what was our present to her?'

'We said that because it was her "twenty-first" birthday, she was grown up at last. So, because she was an adult, it was all right for her to go abroad. We said we would pay for a trip to Switzerland to see Frederick.'

'And when did she go to Switzerland?'

'Well, she couldn't go that year for some reason. Then next year, she went into hospital. That's right. Then the year after that she came to stay with us. She said she didn't feel like travelling. But finally, Frederick persuaded her, and she went out . . . that's right . . . she went to Switzerland on . . .'

She looked at Paul, suddenly realizing what he was getting at.

'That's right, Janet. She flew to Geneva on her twenty-second birthday. We drove her to the airport, remember?'

Paul handed her the piece of paper.

'Look at that.'

The paper had a list of dates on it:

February 29, 1896	Grandma was born.
February 29, 1980	Grandma's '21st' birthday party.
February 29, 1984	Grandma flew to Geneva.
February 1986	Grandma died.
February 29, 1988	Postcard was date stamped at Bedford PO.

Janet looked at her husband and shivered. She felt very cold.

'Forget the postcard, Paul. Throw it away. Please.'

Out of the Way

Edward Bell looked at his watch for the twentieth time.

'The train's late,' he said.

At that moment he heard a station announcement.

'The 12.35 to Peterborough is forty minutes late. We are sorry about this.'

Edward was angry.

'I shall be late for my meeting. And they are sorry!'

He looked along the railway line. Nothing. He decided to walk to the end of the platform. At the end of the platform Edward saw a boy. He was about eighteen years old. He was standing alone and had a notebook in his hand. A train went past. The boy watched it and then wrote something in the notebook. Another train went through the station. The boy made another note in his notebook.

'Are you train spotting?' asked Edward.

The boy jumped. He had not noticed Edward. He nodded. His long fair hair fell across his forehead.

'I used to go train spotting when I was a boy,' said Edward. 'Of course, in those days, trains had names. Now they only have numbers, don't they?'

'S-s-some tr-tr-tr . . . Some trains s-still have a n-n- . . . er still have a n-n- . . . er still have n-names,' said the boy.

He had a terrible stutter. Edward felt sorry for him. The boy's open face and his fair hair made him seem very young. With his stutter, he was even more childlike.

'Really, I didn't know that,' said Edward. 'I thought they only had numbers nowadays. Have you had a good morning?'

Out of the Way

The boy nodded.

'V-v-v . . . er . . . Very good. At least th-th-thirteen new . . . er . . . new ones.'

Edward smiled.

'Will you stay here all day?'

'N-no, I'm going to P-P-P . . . er to . . . er P- . . .'

'Peterborough?' said Edward, trying to help.

The boy nodded.

'So am I,' said Edward. 'We can travel together if you like.'

They sat together on the train to Peterborough. The boy stuttered, but Edward enjoyed their conversation.

'I'm Edward Bell.'

'My name's Br- . . . er Brian. Brian Jackson.'

Edward found out that Brian was nineteen. He worked in a butcher's shop, and he always went train spotting on his day off.

'Do you have any other hobbies?'

'Oh yes! I collect . . . er . . . I collect th-things.'

'You mean things like model cars?'

'Yes. Model cars.'

'So do I!' said Edward. Edward was like many men. He still had a schoolboy's love of model cars.

'Do you live in Peterborough, Brian?'

'Yes. I live in Eastfield Road. D-d-do you kn . . . Do you know it?'

'Yes,' Edward said, 'it's near the market, isn't it? Perhaps I can come to your house and see your collection.'

Edward knocked on the door and waited. He was carrying a small package.

'I hope he likes it,' Edward thought.

A short, grey-haired woman opened the door. Edward looked down at her, feeling uncomfortable.

'Hello. Mrs Jackson?'

'Yes. What do you want? Who are you?'

She did not like strangers at her door.

'Hello, Mrs Jackson. I'm a friend of Brian's. That is, we both collect model cars. I've brought him a car for his collection.'

She looked at the package, but did not invite Edward in.

'Is Brian at home? May I speak to him?'

At that moment Brian came to the door, looking over his mother's shoulder.

'Hello, Brian. Do you remember me? We met on the train. I said I would come to see you. I've brought you a model car for your collection.'

Brian took the package.

'Please c-c-c- . . .'

'Come in,' said the old woman. 'He means he wants you to come in.'

She was very unfriendly, and Edward felt very uncomfortable, but he smiled at her anyway.

'Thank you, Mrs Jackson.'

He turned to Brian.

'I'd love to see your collection, Brian. Could I see it?'

The boy looked at his mother, then he nodded and left the room. Edward did not know whether he should follow Brian or not.

'Sit down, Mr er . . . Have a cup of tea,' said the old woman. It was not an invitation; it was an order. When they were sitting and drinking tea Edward tried to make conversation, but it was not easy.

'Brian's a very nice boy. I'm sure you are proud of him.'

'Hmf. He should stop playing with toys and get a proper job. Butcher's boy. Pah! What kind of job is that?'

'But he seems to like his work.'

'Work! I don't call it work. I wanted him to be an engineer like his father.'

'Ah, Mr Jackson is an engineer?'

'Was.'

'Was? Oh, I see. Mr Jackson's . . .'

'. . . out of the way.'

Out of the Way

Edward did not know what to say. It was such a strange expression: 'out of the way'. What did she mean? Did she mean that he was not at home? Did she mean that he had left her? Did she mean that he was dead? Edward tried a different question.

'So just you and Brian live here? It's a very nice house.'

'Too big for two people,' she said.

That told him what he wanted to know. Brian came back into the room. He looked at his mother before speaking.

'Would you l-l-like to c-c-come . . .'

'Go on, Mr er . . .,' said the old woman. 'Go up and see his silly collection. But don't be too long.'

Brian's room was an amazing place. There were models everywhere. There were models on the bedside table, on the shelves, on the floor, and even on the bed. And there were pictures on every wall.

'I see you like military things, too, Brian.'

'Yes! I've got tanks. And battleships. And guns. I love guns.'

As he spoke, he became more excited. He was not stuttering any more.

'And fighter planes. And rockets. I love anything to do with fighting.'

Edward looked at the boy's open face and his long fair hair. There was nothing childlike about him now. Edward wanted to leave. He had seen enough.

'I want you to see the best part of my collection!' the boy said. 'Look!' He opened a drawer. It was full of knives. All sorts of soldiers' knives. Terrible knives. Knives that kill. He picked one up and waved it under Edward's nose.

'Look at this one! Isn't it beautiful? It's the best knife in my collection.'

He lowered his voice.

'This knife could kill a man. Think of that! It's my knife, and it could kill a man!'

His eyes were bright. He was holding the knife very tightly.

'I must go now, Brian,' Edward said nervously. 'Thank you for showing me your collection.'

Mrs Jackson met Edward at the bottom of the stairs.

'All those silly toys. What a waste of time and money!' she said.

'But those knives, Mrs Jackson. Those knives are not toys. They are very dangerous.'

Edward saw the look in her eyes. The woman was afraid.

'I know,' she said in a whisper, 'but what can I do about it? I cannot stop him. His father tried to stop him and look what happened . . .'

'Mr Jackson? Where is he? You said he was . . .'

'Yes, he's out of the way. I miss him. But Brian doesn't. He always wanted his father out of the way.'

Edward turned and left the house quickly. He didn't stop to say goodbye.

Nice and Warm

'Where's my morning newspaper, Muff? You know I always like to read the newspaper in bed. Can't you do anything right?'

'Sorry, dearest, I forgot. I'll go and get it for you.'

Mrs Muff made a face.

'Oh, it doesn't matter. You'll probably fall down the stairs or something. Ugh! This tea is cold! I hate cold tea! You can't do anything right, can you, Muff?'

'Sorry, dearest. I'll go downstairs and make another cup of tea for you.'

As Muff left the bedroom, she shouted after him:

'... and don't burn the toast!'

'I won't, dear.'

This morning was no different from all the other mornings of the long years of marriage. When they first met and fell in love she was a strong and healthy young woman, but soon after their marriage she became an invalid. The doctor did not really know what was wrong with her. Mrs Muff always said that all her problems were caused by her 'weak nerves'. She spent a lot of her time in bed, either getting better from an old illness or starting a new one. The couple had no children, so Muff had to look after her.

Muff came upstairs carrying a tray with a fresh cup of tea and some toast on it. She looked at the tray.

'Hm. Well, at least you didn't burn the toast, Muff.'

'No, dear. I hope your tea is all right.'

The Penguin Book of Elementary Very Short Stories

Mrs Muff looked at the tray and then at her husband.

'Oh no! Muff, I've told you a thousand times not to wear that stupid red hat. You do it just to upset me, don't you? It makes me ill just to look at it. Take it off!'

She fell back on the pillows as if Muff's red woollen hat had taken away all her strength.

'I'm sorry, dearest. I forgot.'

Muff took off the hat and put it in his pocket. It was only a small hat, like the *kipa* that religious Jews wear, but Muff loved it. He felt undressed without it. Every morning he put it on, and every morning his wife made him take it off again.

When breakfast was finished, Mrs Muff gave him a list of things to do – washing and cleaning and shopping. Muff took the tray and the list and went downstairs. He liked doing the housework and the shopping. He was busy, and the days went quickly for him. Yes, the days were all right, but the best part for him was when he took his wife her cup of cocoa at night.

'I've brought your cocoa, dearest. Drink it while it is hot.'

She looked at him for a moment. When she spoke, her voice was soft.

'I'm sorry I was angry with you this morning, Muff. You know it's my nerves. They're very bad at the moment.'

'I know, dearest. You can't help it.'

'What do you mean "I can't help it"?'

He knew he had said the wrong thing.

'I just meant . . .'

'I know what you meant! You hate me really, don't you, Muff? You think I *like* being ill, you think I *enjoy* having to stay in bed while you go out and meet people and walk in the sunshine and . . . and . . . You'll only be happy when I'm dead, won't you, Muff?'

Her eyes were wet with tears.

'Now, now, dearest,' said Muff. 'Don't upset yourself. Drink your cocoa, and take your sleeping pill. You'll feel better in the morning.'

He picked up the bottle from the bedside table. It was full of

Nice and Warm

bright red pills. He gave it to her. She took out two pills and swallowed them.

'You're lucky, Muff. You just close your eyes and you are fast asleep. I have forgotten what it is like to have a good night's sleep.'

But fifteen minutes later, she was fast asleep, her mouth open. Muff looked down at her. He lifted her hand and let it drop. Yes, she was asleep, he was sure. He took his red hat out of his pocket and put it on. Then he stuck his tongue out at her.

'Muff's got his hat on!' he shouted (but not too loudly). 'Muff's got his old red hat on!' he shouted again (a little louder this time). He began to sing the words. Soon he was dancing and jumping round the room. 'Muff's got his old red hat on! Hip! Hip! Hooray!'

He threw his hat into the air, caught it and pushed it under her nose.

'I'll wear this hat if I like, and you can't stop me, my dear Mrs Muff! You can't stop me!'

He laughed, put the hat on the floor and began dancing round it. This was *his* moment, the moment she could not spoil. He looked at her again. Yes, she was asleep. He was safe.

'Hip! Hip! Hooray!' he shouted, throwing his hat into the air. He started to cough. Suddenly, he couldn't breathe, his face went red, he fell to the floor, on top of his hat. Soon the room was silent except for the sound of Mrs Muff snoring.

It was morning. Mrs Muff woke up. She yawned and opened her eyes slowly. She was thirsty. That's what happens when you sleep with your mouth open. She called out.

'Muff!' she called. 'Muff? Where are you? Where's my tea?'

She muttered to herself: 'Muff, he's a lazy devil! I expect he's gone out and forgotten all about me. He just can't do anything right. He's . . .'

She caught sight of the body on the floor. She could see at once that Muff was dead. Slowly, painfully, she got out of bed, for she was a heavy woman. She put on her slippers and shuffled across the room to where he lay. She looked down at him and shook her head.

'Now what have you done, Muff, you silly man?'

She bent down and took his hand in hers. It was stiff and cold. She let it drop to the floor again. Tears began to run down her cheeks.

'Muff, Muff,' she said softly, 'you foolish old man. What have you done now?'

She wiped her eyes and sat down heavily on the floor next to him. She lifted his body as easily as if he were a little child, and held his head against her breast. She stroked his cold cheek and began to talk softly as if she were singing to him.

'You're such a silly man, such a silly man. You could never do anything right, could you, poor Muff? Never do anything right. What are we going to do with you, Muff? Poor Muff, cold, cold, cold.'

As she said these words, she reached out for the red woollen hat which was on the floor beside him. Gently, the way a mother dresses a baby, she put the hat on his head.

'There you are, Muff! That will keep Muff nice and warm, won't it? Nice and warm, Muff. Nice and warm. Muff's a good boy really.'

Black Mud

There is not much to do in Tel Aviv on the Sabbath. So I did what most visitors do: on Friday afternoon I went to a travel agent's to book a coach tour for the following day. Where should I go to, I wondered? Jerusalem? No, I didn't want to visit a city. I wanted fresh air and peace.

'What about Ein Gedi?' said the travel agent.

The picture on the front of the brochure showed a beach scene. I don't usually go to the beach because I have very white skin and I burn easily.

'No, thank you. No sunbathing.'

'Ah, but people don't go to Ein Gedi to sunbathe. They go because it's on the Dead Sea. You must go to the Dead Sea. Everyone does.'

'Why does everyone go to the Dead Sea?' I asked.

'To float in it.'

'You mean, to swim in it?'

'No, it's dangerous to swim in it. You lie on your back and float.'

I remembered something from my schooldays.

'Ah yes. Our geography teacher once told us about the Dead Sea. It's so full of salt that you cannot sink. You just float in it. Is that right?'

'Yes, that's right. You can even lie on your back and read a newspaper!'

'Well, at least it's something different. OK, I'll go.'

*

Early next morning I was on the coach and looking out of the window. Between Tel Aviv and Jerusalem, the landscape was quite pretty, but here and there, there were rusty old tanks lying on their sides. Why were they still there after so many years?

We went through Jerusalem and out into the empty desert. I began to wonder about the trip. Rusty tanks, an empty landscape and a dead sea: it didn't seem much of a tour. But the landscape was not empty. Here and there, I saw young boys looking after herds of goats. The boys were very thin and their clothes were old and torn. Our coach rushed past. They didn't even look up.

When we got to Ein Gedi everybody went into a large building. There was a changing room inside where we put on our bathing costumes. I began to wish that I had not come. I was already feeling sad because of those poor boys in the desert. Now I felt ashamed of my milk-white skin. I waited until the others had left. Then I walked down the beach towards the water.

The beach was crowded. Most of the people were either couples or families with noisy young children. They were all doing something very strange: they were taking thick black mud from big tubs and putting it over each other's bodies! As soon as they were covered in mud, they went into the water. I couldn't believe my eyes. Why were they doing that? It seemed a crazy thing to do. I began to feel more cheerful. I decided to cover my body with the mud. The mud felt strange but pleasant. It was like oil, and cool on my skin. I tried to put mud on my back as well, but I couldn't reach. What a pity I was alone.

'What are you doing?'

I looked up to see a tall man in swimming trunks. He was a black man, I mean a real black man. His accent was American. I learned later that he was a soldier on leave.

'I'm doing what everyone else is doing,' I said. 'I am covering myself with this black mud.'

Black Mud

It sounded stupid when I said it.

'I can see that. But why are you all doing that?'

'I don't know,' I said, feeling even more stupid. 'Perhaps it is good for the skin.'

'Well, if it's good for your skin, I guess it will be good for mine!' he said. He put his hands into the tub and started to cover himself in mud.

'You've missed some places on your back,' he said.

I nodded, then looked at his back.

'So have you,' I said. 'At least, I think you have!'

We put mud on each other's backs and walked together into the water.

'Don't try to swim in it,' I said. 'It's dangerous to put your face in the water. Just lie back.'

My geography teacher was right. We lay back in the water and floated. It felt great. There we were – two black bodies side by side under the hot Middle Eastern sun. All around us, people were enjoying themselves. Some were standing in the water. Others were floating. Others were washing the mud off. I didn't want to do that. I felt safe under my coat of mud: I was happy with my black body. The world had become a peaceful place. My new friend looked at me and smiled.

'It suits you,' he said. 'Black suits you.' Then he laughed. 'Perhaps it won't come off! Then you'll have a problem, won't you?'

I closed my eyes and almost fell asleep. Peace.

'All good things must come to an end!' he said suddenly.

I opened my eyes again. The sunlight was very strong. It hurt my eyes. I looked at my new friend. He was washing the mud from his body. I did the same. We came out of the water together and walked up the beach towards the changing room. I was white again, he was still black.

The Orinoco Treasure

My mother often said to me: 'Keep away from women who use too much lipstick. Women with painted lips are dangerous.' I always stare at women who have a lot of lipstick on, but I am afraid of them too.

5 The couple at the next table were interesting: a young woman about my age, twenty-eight or so, and a man of about sixty with grey hair and a short grey beard. The man was drunk. He kept resting his head on the table. Each time he did this, the young woman put her hand under his shoulder and lifted him
10 up. Who was she? His daughter? His nurse? Not his wife, surely? He was so much older than her. Each time she helped him, he pushed her away, and drank some more wine. The waiters and the other customers took no notice.

I kept staring at the woman. She was dressed in red: red skirt,
15 red blouse and red shoes. Even her stockings were red. Her skin against the red was as white as milk. Her mouth was beautiful: painted with lipstick that matched the red of her clothes.

'Welcome, stranger!'

The man was speaking to me. He lifted his glass.

20 '*Salute!* Cheers!' he said. I went red.

'Come and sit with us! Have a drink! Tell us your name. Tell us what you are doing in Rome!'

He was very drunk. He pointed to the woman in red.

'I'm tired of her. She is very boring. Very beautiful but very
25 stupid, aren't you, Sybil?'

The Orinoco Treasure

How could he talk to her like that? I felt sorry for her, but she didn't seem to mind.

'Yes, please join us,' she said, pushing a seat towards me. She spoke Italian with a German accent. I thought of my mother's words: women like this are dangerous.

'So, young man. Say something interesting. Tell me about yourself.'

Before I could speak, his head fell forward on the table again. Sybil looked at me.

'He's tired. Poor darling. He works very hard.'

She put her hand out and touched his hair.

'So,' she said, speaking softly as if she did not want to wake him, 'what are you doing in Rome? Are you on holiday? You don't look like a tourist.'

'I . . . I'm a law student. At the University.'

I felt very shy. She smiled. Her red lips made her teeth look very white.

'That's very interesting. Eduardo is a lawyer too.'

She touched his grey hair again.

'Come on, darling,' she said, lifting him up. 'Eduardo, this young man . . . er . . .'

'Miguel Sanchez.'

'. . . Miguel Sanchez . . . is a law student.'

'I'm pleased to meet you, Miguel Sanchez, Student of Law. Have a glass of wine.'

'He is at the University, dearest,' Sybil added.

Why did she have to call this old man 'darling' and 'dearest' all the time? I didn't like it.

'Miguel Sanchez,' he said, 'is not an Italian name. Are you Spanish?'

'Venezuelan,' I replied. He stared at me. Suddenly he seemed to be very angry.

'It isn't possible!' he said. 'Who sent you here? Who are you?'

He turned to Sybil.

'Did you do this? Why have you brought him here? You . . .!'

The Penguin Book of Elementary Very Short Stories

He got up and ran out of the restaurant. Sybil threw some money on the table to pay the bill, and went after him.

That night I slept badly. I dreamed about red dresses and red lips and a woman's hand touching an old man's grey head. For the next few weeks I kept away from the restaurant. But I couldn't stop thinking about Sybil. Perhaps I was in love with her. One Friday evening I was feeling lonely, so I went back there. Eduardo was sitting alone. I turned to go out again when Eduardo saw me. He shouted to me to join him. To my surprise, he was very friendly.

'Miguel, my friend, how nice to see you again! How are your studies going? Let us have a drink and talk about law.'

We talked for a time about my work at the University. Then he asked me again about where I came from.

'Are you really from Venezuela?'

'Yes.'

'From Caracas?'

'Well, I live in Caracas, but my family come from a little town called Curiapo. I'm sure you have never heard of it.'

'I don't believe it!!'

He was very excited.

'Do you know Curiapo?' I asked him. 'It is a very small place.'

'Of course I know it!' he said in a whisper. 'It is at the mouth of the River Orinoco.'

He looked round the restaurant before he spoke again.

'Miguel, tell me the truth. It is very, very important. How long have you known Sybil?'

'I don't know her. I met her the other night for the first time.'

He shook his head sadly.

'Don't be afraid, my young friend. I'm not angry with you. But please tell me the truth. She brought you here, didn't she? She has told you about the treasure, hasn't she?'

'Treasure, sir? What treasure is that?'

'Don't pretend, Miguel! You know everything. I can see that in your eyes. Sybil has told you everything, hasn't she?'

The Orinoco Treasure

He picked up his glass and drank some more wine.

'Well, perhaps she is right,' he went on. 'Perhaps we need a strong young man like you, one who knows the Orinoco. OK, Miguel, it's agreed. The three of us. I've got the money for the trip, Sybil's got the map, and you know Curiapo.'

He tried to shake my hand.

'I'm sorry, sir, I don't know what you are talking about.'

'Never mind. She is a clever girl. She knows what she's doing.'

Then he looked at me, a little afraid.

'But promise me something, Miguel. Don't go without me! Every night I dream about finding the Orinoco Treasure. All those jewels, all those wonderful diamonds and emeralds . . .'

He was dreaming now. He shook his head.

'Sorry, Miguel. I'm a silly old man. Tell me, has Sybil shown you the map?'

I decided it was better not to reply. At that moment, Sybil arrived. She was dressed in red as usual, and looked even more beautiful.

'Good evening, my dear,' Eduardo said. He touched her back as she sat down. She kissed him on the mouth, then turned to me.

'Hello, Miguel! We didn't expect to see you again.'

'Clever! What a clever girl you are, Sybil! You still pretend that he is a stranger, eh?' Eduardo said, touching his nose and smiling at me.

'Well, I know the truth. Miguel and I have had a long talk. He has agreed to help us. Come! Let us study your father's map and make our plans.'

Sybil took a document out of her handbag. It was indeed a map. I looked at it, expecting it to be hundreds of years old. In fact it was a simple drawing in pencil. It was on cheap office paper. It was no more than fifty years old at the most.

'Did your father draw this map?'

She nodded without looking up. She seemed to be uncomfortable. The map showed the mouth of the River Orinoco and

45

even my little town of Curiapo. It also showed an island in the middle of the estuary.

'You know this island, of course,' said Eduardo.

'I think so. But I've never been to it. Nobody lives there.'

'The treasure is there, my friend, on that island. Isn't that right, Sybil?'

She didn't answer. She didn't look at me, but went on staring at the map. I couldn't decide which of them was mad. Perhaps they were both mad. They talked a lot of nonsense about the trip to Venezuela. They talked about getting a boat to go to the island. My uncle in Curiapo has a boat. I think I promised to telephone him, but I cannot remember. I drank wine and looked at Sybil, wishing she would kiss me the way she had kissed Eduardo. Finally they put me into a taxi and sent me home.

I never saw them again. I soon forgot about them and the map and the Orinoco Treasure. I finished my studies in Rome and returned to Venezuela. I became a successful lawyer in Caracas. My life was good but unexciting. About a year later, I went to Curiapo to visit my family. They told me about the accident. About a month earlier, they said, some fishermen had found the body of an old man on the beach. The newspaper said that he had an Italian passport in his pocket. I was curious. I went to the police station to see a cousin of mine who worked there. He got out the report on the dead man:

Name:	Eduardo Luigi di Rita
Place of birth:	Rome, Italy
Age:	61 years
Profession:	Lawyer
Date of arrival in Venezuela:	unknown
Purpose of visit:	unknown
Cause of death:	drowning
Circumstances of death:	unknown

What about Sybil? There was nothing about a woman. Some

months later, back in Caracas, I noticed a colour photograph in the newspaper. It showed a group of well-known people at an expensive New York nightclub. There was a smiling woman in the middle of the picture. She was wearing a red dress and a lot of expensive jewels: diamonds and emeralds ... She was very beautiful, but she had too much lipstick on. As my mother always said, such women are dangerous. I turned to the sports page, where I found a very interesting article about football.

A Miracle on the Galata Bridge

Leyla carefully wiped God's face with her cloth. It was important to be very gentle. She looked at God's face again. Yes, it was much better. After another hour's work, God's face would be clean and everyone could see it. Then she would have a cup of coffee with the others before returning to her work in the north gallery.

'How's it going, Leyla?'

Her boss, Meral, was standing next to her. Meral looked at the painting.

'Good morning, Meral *hanim*,' Leyla said politely.

'Good morning, Leyla.'

She looked at the girl's work.

'That's very good, Leyla!'

Yes, it was very good. Leyla had rubbed away the whitewash without rubbing away any of the paint underneath. The pink of God's face was perfect.

'Yes, very good, Leyla. Any problems?'

'No, Meral *hanim*, I don't think so. It's just as you said: we have to be very careful.'

'That's right. It doesn't matter how long you take. But don't rub the whitewash too hard. If you do, you might rub off the paint as well. Thank Heavens the Ottomans used whitewash to cover up these Christian paintings! Thank Heavens they didn't use paint!'

Leyla nodded. Although she was a Muslim, she thought that these Christian paintings were very beautiful. She loved the

A Miracle on the Galata Bridge

kind faces of the angels and the saints, and she loved the gold paint round their heads. She wanted to rub away all the whitewash and bring the paintings to life again.

'Do we know what is in the rest of this painting?' she asked Meral.

'No. Perhaps it's another painting of God with His angels standing round Him. But be patient. Do your work well, and you will find out for yourself. *Inşallah!* God willing!'

'*Inşallah!*' murmured Leyla.

During the coffee break, Leyla sat quietly and listened to the others talking. They were all experts, and employed in the Ayasofya museum. She was still a student.

'Well, Selim *bey*,' said one of them, 'how is that terrible painting in the south gallery?'

Selim made a face.

'One gets used to it. But I am tired of all these Christian saints and angels. They all look so miserable!'

'Rubbish!' said another. 'They look serious, because they are standing in front of the throne of God. They are serious, but they are not miserable. In fact, they are happy!'

Selim shook his head.

'I don't agree. If they are happy, why can't they look happy? If you are standing in front of God, you should be happy. Listen. You have seen a lot of saints and angels – we find more under the whitewash every day – but have you ever seen one who is smiling?'

There was a silence. Leyla was shocked. She thought that the angels and the saints had beautiful faces. They were serious, but they were beautiful. She wanted to say something, but she was only a student.

'Come on,' said another, 'we must get back to work or Meral *hanim* will stop smiling at us!'

Leyla went back to her painting on the wall of the north gallery. As the days turned into weeks, more and more of the painting would be seen. Meral *hanim* was right: it was a picture of the throne of God with His angels standing round. And Selim *bey* was right: they were all serious, they did not look happy, even if they were happy inside. The painting was nearly finished now, except for one small corner. She could hardly wait to finish the picture. She picked up a fresh cloth and attacked the whitewash.

Too late! Leyla, who had always been so careful, rubbed too hard, and rubbed away the whitewash and the paint underneath. She looked with horror at the spot. The gold was still around the angel's head, but the angel had no face! She had rubbed out the angel's face!

'Oh, no!' she cried out loud, 'what shall I do? What will Meral *hanim* say?'

It was time to go home. Leyla was too afraid to tell Meral *hanim* what had happened. She packed up her things and went out of Ayasofya without speaking to anyone. She slept badly that night. In her dreams, she saw the faces of angels. They were angry faces, except one, which was blank. This was the worst face of all: no eyes, no nose, no mouth, nothing, and yet it seemed to be angrier than all the others.

Next morning Leyla got up and went to work early. She didn't want any breakfast. She decided to walk to Ayasofya over the Galata Bridge.

'Excuse me, miss,' said a voice behind her. She turned round. She thought she knew the voice, but the man was a stranger. He was a young man, very thin and very pale. Leyla never spoke to men on the street – her mother had taught her that – but this one seemed all right. There was something childlike about him. She looked at his face. Hadn't she seen him somewhere before?

'I'm sorry to bother you, miss,' the stranger said, 'but can you tell me how to get to Ayasofya?'

'I'm going there myself. You can come with me.' Leyla was surprised: she felt very comfortable with the young man. What would her mother say if she heard her?

A Miracle on the Galata Bridge

'That's very kind of you,' said the young man. 'Tell me, what do you do? Are you a teacher?'

Leyla laughed.

'Oh no! I'm just a student.'

'And what do you study?'

'Art.'

He nodded.

'What about you?' she asked.

He did not reply. Perhaps he hadn't heard her. She looked at him again. She was sure she had seen him somewhere before.

'I said: what about you? What do you do?' she asked.

'I'm only visiting Istanbul,' he said. It was not an answer to her question.

'I mean, what is your job? Are you a teacher?'

'You could say that.'

'But you don't come from Istanbul, is that right?'

'That's right.'

'Forgive me, but I feel I have met you before. Are you at the University?'

He smiled at her, a long, sweet smile.

'Perhaps I have seen you at the University,' he said.

They had crossed the bridge now, and were close to Ayasofya.

'You are an excellent student. You will do very well,' he added.

What a strange thing to say, thought Leyla. He sounds more like an old man than a young boy.

'Is that Ayasofya?' he asked.

Leyla nodded.

'So now you know where you are.' She pointed across the square. 'That's the main entrance over there. But I don't think the museum is open until . . .'

She stopped in mid-sentence and looked round. He had gone.

'What a strange boy,' she thought.

*

As Leyla went upstairs to the gallery, the memory of last night returned. She forgot about everything else. Slowly she removed the cloth which covered the painting. There was the face of God, and there were the angels standing round His throne, beautiful as always. He was, after all, her God too. She knew that she had to look at the rubbed-out face of the last angel. She took one last look at the face of God and the serious faces of the other angels and then said a little prayer. Then she looked at the corner of the painting. There he was, the last angel, the one with no face. She stared, not believing her own eyes. There was no sign of the damage! The angel had a face. It was a pale thin face, the face of the young man she had met on the Galata Bridge. There was something else that made Leyla very happy. She ran downstairs. She wanted to tell the others what she had found.

Postscript

If you ever go to Istanbul, go to Ayasofya. It is an interesting place. Go inside, climb the stairs to the north gallery and look at the wall paintings. They all seem to be the same, but if you look carefully, you will see one which is different. In the bottom left hand corner, an angel is smiling. As far as I know, it is the only smiling angel in any painting in any Christian church in the world.

Glossary and Language Practice

All Those Noughts

USEFUL VOCABULARY

Nouns

airport	departure	lid
amount	document	luggage
banknote	export	nought
body	fist	pile
branch	flight	president
briefcase	goods	purse
business	ground	quantity
calculator	handbag	record
case	heart	safe
cash	identity	specialist
clothes	idiot	stairs
counter	import	tax
credit card	kind of	thief
cubicle	knee	tourist
customer	lap	trouble
department store		

Verbs

argue	contain	expect
book	cry out	faint
close	disappear	kill

The Penguin Book of Elementary Very Short Stories

Verbs

miss	realize	sign
notice	reappear	smile
pat	record	spell
pick (pockets)	remember	stare
pick up	rub	steal

Adjectives

afraid	fair	normal
angry	foreign	own
cheap	glad	possible
decent	honest	safe
dishonest	invisible	sick
excited	lovely	smooth
expensive	main	straight

Others

as if	out of sight	suddenly
fast	really	unlike
nowadays		

GLOSSARY

nought (title): 0. Also called 'zero'.

Buy cheap and sell dear (line 11): that is, buy goods at a low price and sell them at a high price.

goods (line 14): the word is always plural.

he patted his briefcase (line 16): you would pat a child or a pet such as a dog to show that you loved it.

he got Swiss papers (line 32): 'papers' means all the documents he needed to be able to live and work in Switzerland (e.g., identity card, work permit).

picking pockets (line 33): stealing from people by taking things from their pockets.

Little and often (line 34): he believes that it is better to steal small amounts but to steal often.

credit cards (line 39): cards used to buy goods 'on credit', that is, you pay for them later. For example, American Express.

trying the airport (line 41): Dix means that the airport is a good place for thieves.

Glossary and Language Practice

fat (line 42): Dix means that the tourists will have a lot of things worth stealing.

if you ask me (line 43): the same as 'in my opinion'.

I told your office that I would pick my ticket up (line 54): in reported speech, the tense of the verb usually changes when the reporting verb is in the past: 'I *will* pick my ticket up' – He told them he *would* pick his ticket up.

hurry up or I'll miss my flight (line 61): the same as; 'if you don't hurry up, I will miss my flight'.

reappear (line 73): the briefcase had *disappeared*. Sulo hoped that it would *reappear*, i.e., come back (appear again).

Dix would buy that from him (line 79): this is like reported speech. It is what Yanni was thinking: 'Dix will buy that from me' – he thought that Dix would buy it from him.

rubbed his hands (line 85): we rub our hands together to warm them, or when we are going to get something nice.

It's just not fair! (line 103): if things are as they should be, they are fair; if not, they are unfair. For example it is not fair to pay men more than women for the same work.

out of sight (line 103): where nobody would see it.

Yanni's heart stopped (line 110): it means that when he suddenly saw Sulo, he was very frightened.

decent people (line 118): just as Yanni thinks of himself as 'an honest thief', Sulo thinks of himself as 'a decent person'.

LANGUAGE PRACTICE

A

Look at the story again to find answers to these questions:

1 What was Sulo's nationality?
2 How did Sulo become rich?
3 Why do you think Yanni was such a good thief?
4 What do you know about Dix?
5 Why was it so easy for Yanni to steal the briefcase?

B

Put in the missing words. We usually give you the first or last letters of the missing words. You can find all the expressions in the story.

1 Sulo's clothes t_____ you that he was a rich man.

The Penguin Book of Elementary Very Short Stories

2 When he was young, Sulo decided that he wanted to m_____ a lot of money. Before he was twenty, he had his o_____ business.

3 Sulo got rich by buying st_____ goods at a l_____ price and selling them at a _____ price.

4 When he was in the taxi, Sulo didn't put his briefcase on the seat. He carried it _____ his _____.

5 He wondered what would people say if they k_____ he _____ a million dollars in his briefcase.

6 Yanni was g_____ that he was _____ible, because it meant that nobody c_____ remember his face.

7 Yanni got money by p_____ pockets and st_____ purses from h_____.

8 Yanni u_____ to s_____ most of his time at the railway station.

9 Globus is a famous d_____ s_____ in Bahnhofstrasse.

10 Dix was a s_____ in stolen cr_____ c_____ and foreign money.

11 Sulo had put his briefcase on the g_____, and was too busy a_____ with the girl to think about it.

12 Sulo booked his fl_____ at an office in town and arranged to _____ his ticket up at the airport.

13 The girl at the counter had no re_____ of Sulo's b_____.

14 'How do you _____ Sulo?' 'S-U-L-O.'

15 Sulo told the girl to h_____ up, because he didn't want to m_____ his plane to Amsterdam.

16 Someone had _____ a mistake when they took the booking. His ticket was _____ the name Solo, not Sulo.

17 Sulo f_____ sick when he found _____ that his briefcase _____ dis_____.

18 Before he opened the case, Yanni was excited: that is why he r_____ his hands. But when he saw the money, he felt a_____.

19 Yanni was so angry that he hit the l_____ of the briefcase with his f_____.

20 Yanni didn't want _____one to find the briefcase so he put it _____ _____ behind the toilet.

C

Discuss these questions with someone else who has read the story:

1 Sulo's million dollars was all the money he had saved. Do you feel sorry for him? How would you feel if you lost all your savings?

Glossary and Language Practice

2   Why did Yanni leave all the money in the briefcase? What else could he have done? What would you have done?
3   Sulo and Yanni are both dishonest men. Is one just as bad as the other?

Ladybirds

USEFUL VOCABULARY

Nouns

beetle	museum	prize
box	neck	science
cheek	palm (of hand)	spot
horn	piece	wing

Verbs

answer	frown	move
bend	hold	pause
burn	jump	repeat
clap	keep	run away
collect	kneel	scratch
count	laugh	scream
crawl	let go of	shake
disappear	look after	shout
drop	lose	watch
enjoy	mean	whisper
explain	mind (object)	worry

Adjectives

angry	exciting	real
ashamed	famous	scientific
busy	missing	serious
careful	natural	several
central	odd (strange)	shiny
common	out of breath	special
different	pretty	wonderful
excited		

The Penguin Book of Elementary Very Short Stories

Others
at once   it doesn't matter   especially
closely

GLOSSARY

... you can call me Poff. Everybody does. (line 20): we use 'does' instead of repeating the whole phrase 'Everybody *calls me Poff*'.

funny (line 21): 'funny' has two meanings. It means 'amusing', that is, it describes something which makes you laugh. Here, it means 'strange, odd, peculiar', that is, it describes something which you find unusual.

shiny (line 31): a lot of common adjectives are made from nouns and verbs by adding -y, for example, shine/shiny, dirt/dirty, sun/sunny.

May I pick one up? (line 34): 'may' is used to ask permission. We also use 'can': 'Can I pick one up?'

The old man scratched his head (line 48): people scratch their heads when they are not sure what to do or say next.

Rebecca clapped her hands (line 73): she clapped her hands to show that she was excited or pleased.

I don't think your mummy would be very happy if you took a big black beetle into the house (line 76): notice that the word 'not' goes with the verb 'think', that is, we say 'I don't think she would ...', not 'I think she wouldn't ...'.

especially one with horns (line 77): Poff means 'And she certainly wouldn't be happy if you took a beetle with horns into the house.'

See if you can find me some ladybirds (line 84): you could also say 'See if you can find some ladybirds for me'.

Do they have lots and lots of spots? (line 88): children like to repeat words, as here: '*lots and lots* of spots'.

'Got one!' she shouted (line 96): people often leave out the first part of the sentence when they speak. Rebecca means: 'I've got one.'

as much as he did (line 98): that is, 'as much as he loved beetles'.

Well done, Rebecca! (line 99): we say 'well done' to congratulate people, that is, to tell them that they have done something very well.

She shook her head (line 101): you shake your head when you want to say no, or when you do not understand something.

It didn't matter (line 122): it wasn't important if the ladybird was a new species or just a strange one.

I've been looking everywhere for you! (line 142): she uses this form of the verb

Glossary and Language Practice

(the present perfect continuous) to say that the action (looking for Rebecca) started in the past and was still going on until this moment.

at once (line 143): the same as 'immediately' or 'right away'.

As for you, old man (line 144): having shouted at Rebecca, she is now ready to shout at Poff.

LANGUAGE PRACTICE

A

Look at the story again to find answers to these questions:

1 Where was Poff when Rebecca first spoke to him, and what was he doing?
2 Why did Rebecca think that he was 'just like a teacher'?
3 There were several things that Poff liked about Rebecca. What were they?
4 Why didn't Poff answer Rebecca's question 'How many spots do they (ladybirds) have'?
5 Why was Poff so excited about the ladybird that Rebecca found?

B

Put in the missing words. We usually give you the first letters of the missing words. You can find all the expressions in the story.

1 A ladybird is a k_____ of insect. It is red with black s_____ on.
2 Rebecca wanted to know why Poff was down on his h_____ and k_____ in the long grass.
3 She wanted to know if he was looking _____ something.
4 Please _____ _____ your name.
5 Poff doesn't like girls who are sh_____ or s_____. He liked Rebecca because she was not a _____ of beetles.
6 Rebecca thought that 'Poff' was a f_____ name. She didn't think that it was his r_____ name.
7 The box was f_____ of small p_____ of newspaper. Under the paper, there were l_____ and l_____ of sh_____ insects.
8 Rebecca th_____ that they were very pr_____, and she wanted to p_____ one _____.
9 He was gl_____ that she was as interested _____ insects _____ he was.
10 When the insect ran a_____ Rebecca's hand, and d_____ into the grass, she expected Poff to be angry _____ her.

The Penguin Book of Elementary Very Short Stories

11 Poff c_____ insects because he wanted to know as m_____ a_____ their lives as possible.

12 The old man scr_____ his head because he didn't know how to explain to Rebecca why he was so i_____ in beetles.

13 When she looked _____ the box, Rebecca saw that the beetles were of d_____ colours.

14 When her hair t_____ his ch_____, Poff suddenly f_____ very lonely.

15 Poff wanted to look _____ more insects to a_____ to his c_____.

16 Rebecca wanted to k_____ the beetle with the long h_____, but Poff t_____ her to put it in the box with the o_____.

17 He thought that Rebecca's mother _____ not be happy if Rebecca t_____ a big black beetle into the house.

18 The sc_____ name for the ladybird is *Coccinella 7-punctata*. Poff remembered the first time that he _____ counted the seven s_____ on a ladybird.

19 Poff l_____ the little girl a_____ his head and danced until he was out of b_____.

20 The sound of a woman's angry v_____ made them both j_____. It was Rebecca's mother, who said: 'I've _____ l_____ everywhere _____ you, Rebecca!'

C

Discuss these questions with someone else who has also read the story.

1 What is the difference between Poff's and Rebecca's interest in insects? How does he help her to learn about them? Do you think you could become interested in studying insects?

2 What do you learn about Poff's character and his life from this story? Why do you think he liked Rebecca so much? Do you feel sorry for him?

3 Why was Rebecca's mother so angry (a) with Rebecca, (b) with Poff? How would you have reacted if you had been Rebecca's mother?

4 Why did Poff let Rebecca keep the unusual ladybird?

Glossary and Language Practice

The Ninety-piece Man

USEFUL VOCABULARY

Nouns

bill	lorry	side
bottom	machine	situation
camper	method	sky
card	miracle	speed
company	motorway	surprise
cooker	number	telephone
crisis	number-plate	line
decision	pity	telex
director	price	thunder
driver	problem	truth
earthquake	repair	van
fax number	revolution	war
gun	scene	world
idea	service	

Verbs

argue	ignore	see to
change	introduce	shoot
break down	lie back	shrug
buy	mean	speed
fall	mend	stay
happen	owe	travel
hate	refuse	upset
hitchhike	remain	

Adjectives

calm	pleasant	strange
clean	quiet	sure
female	ready	thirsty
foreign	sick	unkind
perfect		

61

The Penguin Book of Elementary Very Short Stories

Others

All right	it won't go	thanks to
By the way	In other words	Well done
certainly	of course	What's the matter?
Excuse me	at high speed	

GLOSSARY

a camper (line 5): a van in which you can go camping.

James, you can't be serious! (line 7): she doesn't believe him. She thinks that he is joking.

Katy will get you and me and the children to Italy (line 8): 'get' here means 'take' or 'carry'.

K – T. Kay – tee. Katy (line 12): Katy is the short form of the girl's name 'Kathleen' or 'Catherine'.

in the middle of nowhere (line 13): a fixed expression. Sue means that they will not know where they are.

She's a good van (line 22): men often refer to such things as their car or their boat as 'she'.

blah blah blah blah (line 37): this is used to show words you do not understand or are not interested in.

In other words, no (line 45): Sue means: 'What you are really saying is, no.'

This van is sick. If it was a horse, you would shoot it (line 59): 'sick' means 'ill'.

Buona sera, signori! Posso aiutarvi? (line 65) 'Good evening! Can I help you?'

Scusi, signora, non capisco (line 72): I'm sorry, I don't understand'

It's a pity you can't speak English either! (line 85): to Sue, his technical explanation is more like a foreign language than English.

At your service (line 97): in full: 'I am at your service' meaning 'Tell me how I can help you.'

Dott. (line 99): short for Dottore, the Italian word for Doctor.

It won't go (line 106): the same as 'it has broken down'.

a mechanic to see to it (line 110): the mechanic will find out what is wrong and will then put it right.

argued (line 126): almost the same as 'quarrelled'.

her face as black as thunder (line 134): her face showed that she was very angry.

Good! Wonderful! What an exciting holiday! (line 140): Sue is being sarcastic, saying the opposite of what she is feeling.

hitchhike (line 143): hitchhikers stand by the side of the road and point along it with their thumbs to let motorists know that they want a lift. Motorists

Glossary and Language Practice

usually respond by ignoring them. It is therefore a mystery how so many hitchhikers get to where they want to go.

The mechanic shrugged (line 155): when you meet a problem which you cannot solve, you shrug, that is, you raise your shoulders (and often your hands and your eyebrows as well). This makes you feel better and everyone else a lot worse.

He is a friend of ours (line 171): it is similar to 'He is one of our friends'. This pattern 's/he is a friend of mine/ours/yours' is much commoner than 's/he is my friend'.

His mouth fell open (line 172): this shows that he was surprised, or afraid.

LANGUAGE PRACTICE

A

Look at the story again to find answers to these questions:

1 Sue doesn't like the idea of going to Italy in the van. What is she afraid of?
2 Why did James call the van Katy? What did Sue think of the name?
3 When the van broke down the first time, Sue compared it to a horse. What did she mean?
4 When the van broke down a second time, how did they manage to find a mechanic?
5 How did the second mechanic react when he saw Donzelli's card? Why did he react in this way?

B

Put in the missing words. We usually give you the first or last letters of the missing words. You can find all the expressions in the story.

1 When Sue thought that James was joking, she said: 'James, you _____ be serious!' He replied: 'Of course I'm serious. Katy will _____ us to Italy.'
2 James called the van Katy because of the letters on the n_____ p_____.
3 Sue r_____ to call the van 'Katy', because it was c_____ not f_____.
4 'I have _____ i_____ what you're _____ing about. J_____ tell me one thing: can you m_____ it?'
5 James decided to _____ the truth.

63

The Penguin Book of Elementary Very Short Stories

6 Sue said: 'This van is ___ ___ck. If it ___ a horse, you ___ sh___ it.'
7 When she spoke to the driver, Sue spoke very ___ly. The driver listened ___ly. He liked the way the English people were always so c___ in a cr___.
8 It was very k___ of the mechanic to r___ to take ___ money.
9 Sue was very angry: her face was as ___ as ___.
10 James decided to h___ to the n___ town to ___ a mechanic.
11 James did not have ___ money to ___ the bill.
12 When James said the bill was too much, the mechanic shr___ his sh___ and smiled.

C

Supply the missing words. They are mostly prepositions.

1 Sue stared ___ the white van. Then she turned ___ her husband.
2 I don't want to travel ___ Europe ___ this van. What happens if it breaks ___?
3 *Autostrada* is Italian ___ 'motorway'.
4 James was ___ the van, trying to find ___ what was wrong. On the autostrada, cars and lorries went past ___ high speed.
5 I have no idea what you're talking ___.
6 James sat ___ ___ the grass, lay ___ and closed his eyes.
7 The driver got ___ ___ the car and came ___ ___ them.
8 Donzelli promised to send a mechanic to see ___ the van.
9 I told you there was nothing to worry ___.
10 The mechanic turned ___ Sue and began to shout ___ her ___ Italian.
11 Mr Donzelli is a friend ___ ours.
12 He handed the card ___ ___ Sue.

D

Discuss these questions with someone else who has also read the story.

1 What do you think of the idea of a family holiday in a VW camper? What are the good points and the bad points about such a holiday?

Glossary and Language Practice

2 What have you learned from the story about the character of (a) James (b) Sue? Are you more like Sue or more like James?
3 Does this story really tell you anything about the English 'character' and the Italian 'character'? Would it matter if the nationality of the family and the holiday country were different?

This Bed is Cold

USEFUL VOCABULARY

Nouns

back	makeup	rubbish
darling	mummy	shoulder
fool	neck	skin
hope	party	suitcase
husband	peace	type
liar	perfume	voice
life	problem	

Verbs

brush	ignore	shine
care	interest	smell
close	leave	steal
decide	let go	suffer
find out	lie	suppose
follow	pack	touch
get away from	prefer	try
get back (return)	quarrel	wear
hate	seem	win
hide		

Adjectives

calm	guilty	smooth
casual	horrible	sorry
difficult	jealous	typical
front	naughty	wonderful
gentle	shocked	

The Penguin Book of Elementary Very Short Stories

Others

as (when)	finally	not even
on business	it doesn't matter	usually
downstairs		

GLOSSARY

It seems days ago (line 3): that is, it seems as if he left days ago.

I saw the way he looked at her (line 7): the same as: I saw how he looked at her.

Typical man! (line 8): he behaves as all men behave.

I just wanted to know where he had been (line 12): 'just' is often used like this. It means 'I only wanted...', or 'that is all I wanted...'

the States (line 17): a short form of the United States of America.

on business (line 17): there are many expressions with the pattern preposition + noun, without the article 'the', for example, go to school, be in bed, travel by train.

I used to love that (line 34): 'used to' + infinitive describes something which happened regularly in the past, but no longer happens. 'I used to smoke a lot, but now I don't smoke at all.'

naughty (line 43): the word 'naughty' is used about children who have done something wrong.

What does he see in her? (line 51): what does he find attractive about her?

makeup (line 52): the general word for all the cosmetics that a woman uses on her face: lipstick, eye-shadow, mascara, face powder, etc.

His voice is always so smooth when he lies (line 67): she uses the word 'smooth' to suggest that he spoke carefully to hide the fact that he was lying.

mummy (line 77): she uses the children's word for mother to emphasize that he is behaving like a little boy.

But it didn't work (line 79): that is, it wasn't successful.

He's come back! I knew he would (line 80): in full: 'He has come back. I knew (that) he would come back.'

Why should I? (line 83): in full: 'Why should I brush my hair?'

Let him take me as I am (line 83): that is, he must accept me as I am.

LANGUAGE PRACTICE

A

Look at the story again to find answers to these questions:

1 What reason does the husband give for being late?

Glossary and Language Practice

2 What, according to his wife, was the real reason why he was late?
3 How does she react when he comes into the kitchen and tries to kiss the back of her neck?
4 When she hears the front door and realizes that he has come back, is she pleased? What does she decide to do?
5 Is this the first time she and her husband have quarrelled? How do you know?

B

Put in the missing words. We usually give you the first or last letters of the missing words. You can find all the expressions in the story.

1 It was the m_____ of summer and the sun _____ _____ ing.
2 The other woman is horrible because she _____ to st_____ other _____'s husbands.
3 It is t_____ of men to r_____ after every woman who smiles _____ them.
4 She was angry because her husband _____ come h_____ l_____. She was j_____ because she thought he _____ b_____ with another woman.
5 He m_____ Bill Brown and they went _____ _____ dr_____.
6 She knew that her husband was l_____ because she could sm_____ a woman's p_____ on him.
7 Bill Brown had been to the _____ _____ business.
8 I u_____ to love the w_____ he kissed me, but I don't love it _____ more.
9 Her husband tried to h_____ the tr_____ from her, but she found _____ anyway.
10 Please l_____ me a_____: I don't want to talk to you.
11 You know when children have been n_____y, because they always look so g_____y.
12 Some women put too much m_____ on their faces.

C

All these irregular verbs are used in the story. Can you complete this table?

know	I knew	I have known
come	_____	_____
feel	_____	_____
find	_____	_____

The Penguin Book of Elementary Very Short Stories

get	_____	_____
go	_____	_____
hear	_____	_____
make	_____	_____
meet	_____	_____
put	_____	_____
run	_____	_____
say	_____	_____
see	_____	_____
shine	_____	_____
speak	_____	_____
steal	_____	_____
tell	_____	_____
think	_____	_____
wear	_____	_____

D

Discuss these questions with someone else who has also read the story.

1 In this story, who do you believe: the wife or the husband? Why?
2 She says 'Men are little boys'. What examples does she give? Do you agree with her?
3 If you are jealous, does this mean that you love the other person very much? Are you a jealous type?

The Sorry Joke

USEFUL VOCABULARY

Nouns

barracks	diary	event
belt	direction	expert
brick	dozen	guide
cemetery	drumbeat	hut
chimney	engine	independence
church	escape	jacket

Glossary and Language Practice

Nouns

joke	Muslim	slave
key	pair	slave trader
knowledge	postcard	soldier
labourer	prison	stick
land	proverb	stone
leaf	quarters	throat
leather	queen	tip (money)
madman	remains	title
master	revenge	tower
message	rope	translation
minaret	ruins	village
mirror	scrap of paper	warning
mosque	site	

Verbs

announce	dig	point out
blow down	form	save
build	insult	set off
bury	lead	shiver
clear	lock	signal
cut	obey	sneeze
deserve	offer	sound like
die		

Adjectives

amazed at	hopeless	public
blind	huge	rusty
colonial	independent	simple
concerned	overhanging	terrible
cruel	made of	torn
fascinating	proud of	unwilling
holy		

Others

As a matter of fact	certainly	in charge of
As far as X is concerned		

GLOSSARY

As a matter of fact I'm Swedish (line 8): we use the expression 'As a matter of

The Penguin Book of Elementary Very Short Stories

fact' to make a true statement which is different from what the other person might have expected.

There were dozens of scraps of paper (line 72): a dozen is literally twelve, but we use 'dozens of' to mean 'lots of'. Similarly, 'scores of' from 'score', which is literally twenty.

all over the world (line 75): a fixed expression meaning everywhere in the world.

Kejeri's finger moved from left to right over the letters. 'Professor' Kejeri does not know everything, thought Tor (line 100): Arabic writing, of course, goes from right to left. Kejeri knew it was Arabic writing, but obviously he couldn't read it.

the remains of a chimney (line 105): that is, what was left of a chimney. The word 'remains' is used only in the plural (compare 'goods' in Story 1) (line 14) and 'barracks' (in line 113).

In the country of the blind, the one-eyed man is king (line 109): 'the blind' here is plural; it means 'blind people'. In a country where everyone is blind, a man who could see, even if he had only one eye, would be very important.

Tor cleared his throat (line 143): *Ahem* (line 145): he coughed a little before he spoke. 'Ahem!' is the sound you make when you clear your throat.

LANGUAGE PRACTICE

A

Say what is wrong with the following statements

1 Kejeri thought that Tor came from Stockholm.
2 Tor invited Kejeri to come with him to Kaole.
3 Tor was impressed by Kejeri's office.
4 Kejeri had trained in London with Professor Roy Williams.
5 The letters and cards in Kejeri's diary were from Britain.
6 The ruined minaret was part of a mosque.
7 Kejeri could read Arabic but he couldn't write it.
8 The slave traders came originally from Baluchistan.
9 The Hanging Tree is still used by the Tanzanian police.
10 Tor gave Kejeri some money for being such a good guide.

B

Put in the missing words. We usually give you the first or last letters of the missing words. You can find all the expressions in the story.

1 Kejeri w_____ a jacket and a p_____ of old, torn trousers.

Glossary and Language Practice

2. His hat was made _____ l_____ and was e_____ n older _____ his trousers.
3. Tor replied: 'No, I am not British. As a m_____ of _____ I'm Swedish.'
4. Kejeri cl_____ into the van. Then Tor st_____ up the engine and s_____ off in the d_____ of Kaole.
5. Professor Williams left the country shortly after In_____, leaving Kejeri in ch_____ of the site.
6. Kejeri's hut was _____ of st_____s and banana l_____s and looked _____ if it _____ blow down if you sn_____ near it.
7. Kejeri had a r_____y key in his pocket, and a h_____ knife hanging _____ his b_____.
8. Kejeri t_____ the key _____ his pocket and un_____ the door.
9. In Kejeri's d_____y, there were d_____s of sc_____s of paper, mostly business c_____ and letters from _____ _____ the world.
10. At Kaole you can still see the c_____y where people are buried.

C

Fill in the missing words. In some cases, several different words will fit. Look at the text to see how well you have done.

They drove back past the village _____ the Baluchis still lived, past the old _____ where the slaves were held. Suddenly, Kejeri _____ to Tor to stop.

'Look there, sir.'

He was _____ to a tree with overhanging _____.

'That is the "Hanging Tree", sir. _____ colonial times, prisoners were hanged there, in _____ of all the people.'

'_____ hangings?'

'Yes, sir. It was a _____. In colonial times, the people in _____ said: "We are the _____ here. You must obey our _____."'

Tor did not know _____ to say.

'There were many laws, _____. Many prisoners. Many hangings in _____ days. See where the rope has cut _____ the branch.'

D

Discuss these questions with someone else who has also read the story.

1. What do you learn from the story about the character and life of (a) Tor

71

The Penguin Book of Elementary Very Short Stories

and (b) Samahani Kejeri? Which one would you prefer to spend a day with?
2 What does the story tell us about the colonial period in this part of Africa? Did colonialism do any good at all?
3 Why did Tor drive away without even saying goodbye? What do you think Kejeri was waiting for? What would you have done if you had been Tor?

A Postcard from Grandma

USEFUL VOCABULARY

Nouns

adult	grandma	mystery
birthday	handwriting	novel
countryside	information	postmark
detective	joke	present
diary	letterbox	rate
drawer	list	reason
explanation	meal	sheet (of paper)
fault	member	signature
grandchild	message	trip

Verbs

believe	knock	realize
explain	make sense	shiver
feel like	pause	stay
get at = mean	persuade	wonder
hand	print	

Adjectives

cruel	liable	upset
grown up	unmarried	

Others

abroad	except for	Thank goodness
at last	in case	What on earth . . .?
exactly		

Glossary and Language Practice

GLOSSARY

LIABLE TO SECOND CLASS RATE (illustration): this means that the postcard has no stamp on it, and that the person who receives the postcard must pay the postage.

lovely day (line 14): the English are well-known for talking about the weather. He means 'It's a lovely (fine) day today, isn't it?'

all he had in his hand was a postcard (line 18): 'all he had' here means 'the only thing that he had'. Other examples: 'All you need is love' (a Beatles song); 'All I want is a quiet life'.

I'm afraid . . . (line 20): we use this expression to say that we are sorry to give someone bad news.

Who on earth . . . (line 31): we use 'on earth' after question words like 'How?', 'What?' and 'Where?' to express surprise or anger: 'How on earth did you know I was a Gemini?' 'What on earth is that red mark on your hand?' 'Where on earth have you been?'

Thank goodness . . . (line 36): also 'Thank Heavens' or 'Thank God'. We thank God that a bad situation will get or has got better.

Grandma (line 37): a child's word for grandmother. Also 'granny' or 'nanna'.

little (line 38): that is, very young.

No, love . . . (line 54): Paul calls his wife 'love'. It is a word of affection. It means the same as 'darling' or 'dear'.

it just doesn't make sense! (line 73): that is, it is a mystery, there is no explanation.

for some reason (line 107): that is, for a reason that I don't know.

realizing what he was getting at (line 112): Janet finally understood the point that Paul was making.

We drove her to the airport . . . (line 114): that is, 'We took her to the airport in the car.'

LANGUAGE PRACTICE

A

Look at the story again to find answers to these questions:

1. Why did Mrs Jones need to give the postman 48p?
2. What made Mrs Jones 'go white' (line 34)?
3. How could Paul be so sure that the postcard was from his mother?
4. Grandma's trip to Switzerland was made in 1980 but she didn't go until four years later. Why not?
5. What was the family joke about grandma's age?

The Penguin Book of Elementary Very Short Stories

B

Put in the missing words. We usually give you the first or last letters of the missing words. You can find all the expressions in the story.

1 The story of grandma's postcard is a real m_____y.
2 The card was in grandma's h_____ing, it was grandma's sig_____ a the bottom, but nobody could understand the _____ge. None of made s_____.
3 _____ morning in e_____y March the postman kn_____ _____ the door of the Joneses' house in Admaston.
4 Mrs Jones said sorry _____ _____ it were her f_____ there wa no stamp _____ the postcard.
5 She had to pay more _____ usual for the stamp because the postcar was _____ a _____d.
6 She wondered who _____ _____th had s_____ them a postcar _____ Switzerland.
7 'Th_____ _____ness Paul will be b_____ soon!' she said.
8 Was it really a postcard _____ grandma, or was it a cr_____ joke?
9 She couldn't have left it in a dr_____ in a hotel because she didn st_____ in a hotel.
10 Paul p_____ his wife _____ _____ arm and told her not t _____ up _____.

C

Fill in the missing words. In some cases, several different words will fit. Look at th text to see how well you have done.

The same evening, Paul _____ a long time looking _____ the postcarc He took _____ a piece of paper _____ wrote down every _____ tha was on the postcard, printed or _____. He looked at his old _____, h read old letters _____ members of his family. He _____ telephone several people who _____ have useful information. Finally, he _____ ou a clean sheet of _____ and made a short _____. Then he _____ t Janet.

D

Discuss this question with someone else who has also read the story.

This is a true story. A man and his wife received this postcard a few years agc The words on it are exactly as given in the story (except for the names and th

Glossary and Language Practice

address). They have discussed the postcard many times, but still cannot explain the mystery. What do you think?

Out of the Way

USEFUL VOCABULARY

Nouns

announcement	gun	platform
battleship	hobby	rocket
bedside	invitation	shelf
conversation	kind of	sort of
day off	market	station
drawer	military	tank
engineer	model	toy
expression	notebook	train spotting
fighter plane	order	waste
forehead	package	whisper

Verbs

be long (time)	grow up	lower
collect	invite	stutter
fight	kill	wave

Adjectives

amazing	late	proud of
childlike	nervous	silly
fair	proper	tight

Others

abroad	anyway	really
along	nowadays	

GLOSSARY

train spotting (line 14): 'train spotting' is the name of the hobby. You 'spot', that is, see, trains and note down details about them, such as name, number and type.

in those days (line 18): that is, when Edward was a boy.

The Penguin Book of Elementary Very Short Stories

childlike (line 24): that is, very young, like a child.

on his day off (line 41): that is, on his free day, when he does not have to work. Another example: 'I'm taking all next week off so that I can go to Liverpool to see my parents.'

I'm a friend of Brian's (line 62): the same pattern as 'a friend of mine/yours/ours/etc.' If Edward had said 'I am Brian's friend', it would suggest either that Brian had only one friend, or that there was something very special about the friendship between Edward and Brian.

anyway (line 77): that is, he smiled at her even though (in spite of the fact that) she was unfriendly.

a proper job (line 89): she thinks that being a butcher's boy is not a proper, that is, a serious or good job.

before speaking (line 106): the same as 'before he spoke'.

But don't be too long (line 109): that is, 'don't take a long time'.

LANGUAGE PRACTICE

A

What is wrong with these statements?

1 Edward met Brian on the platform of Peterborough station.
2 Brian wrote down the names of all the trains that went through the station.
3 Edward lived in the same street as Brian.
4 Edward went to see Brian to give him a model train to add to his collection.
5 Mrs Jackson took Edward upstairs to see her son's collection.
6 Brian told Edward that he had always wanted to be a soldier like his father.
7 Brian's mother was pleased that her son had such a nice hobby.
8 Edward was surprised when he saw how tidy Brian's room was.
9 Edward asked Brian to show him his collection of military knives.
10 Mrs Jackson explained to Edward that Brian missed his father very much.

B

Choose the correct word. Go back to the text to check your answers.

1 Brian's room was an amazing/amazed place.
2 As he spoke/told about his collection, Brian became more and more exciting/excited.

Glossary and Language Practice

3 Edward thought it/there was something very childish/childlike about Brian.
4 Trains used to have/having names, but in those days/nowadays most trains only have numbers.
5 Brian always went train spotting in/on his day off/out.
6 Edward explained/told that he was a friend of Brian's/Brian's friend.
7 Edward found it difficult to make/have conversation to/with Mrs Jackson.
8 Mrs Jackson thought that Brian's toys are/were a waste/loss of time and money.
9 She said/told Edward how much she missed/lost her husband.
10 Edward left without even to say/saying goodbye.

C

Discuss these questions with someone else who has also read the story.

1 What do you learn from this story about the life and character of (a) Brian; (b) Brian's parents?
2 Mrs Jackson said that her husband was 'out of the way'. What do you think really happened to him? Why?
3 Many hobbies are about collecting things (train numbers, stamps, matchbox labels, etc.). Why is collecting so popular? Is it more popular with boys than with girls? Why?

Nice and Warm

USEFUL VOCABULARY

Nouns

bedside	marriage	stairs
breast	nerves	strength
devil	pill	tear
floor	pillows	toast
housework	sleeping pill	top
invalid	slippers	tray

Verbs

bend	call out	catch sight of
breathe	catch	cough

The Penguin Book of Elementary Very Short Stories

Verbs

dress	make a face	spoil
drop	mutter	stick out
fall	pick up	stroke
fall in love	reach	swallow
happen	shuffle	wipe
lift	snore	yawn

Adjectives

foolish	lazy	religious
fresh	lucky	stiff
healthy	painful	woollen
ill		

Others

at least	fast asleep	probably
beside	Hip! Hip! Hooray!	upstairs

GLOSSARY

Nice and warm (title): the expression 'nice and + adjective' means 'very' to describe something which is good. Other examples: 'Eat your dinner while it's nice and hot.' 'Try to keep your room nice and tidy.'

I'll go and get it for you (line 4): here, get means fetch.

Mrs Muff made a face (line 5): you 'make a face' to show that you don't like something.

fall down the stairs or something (line 6): 'or something' means 'or something like that, I'm not sure what'. Another example: 'A man came to the house the other day. He was selling insurance or something.'

Ugh! (line 7): a noise you make to show that you dislike something very much. For example, you might say 'Ugh!' if you were eating an apple and found a worm in it. (You would *certainly* say 'Ugh!' if you found half a worm in it).

an invalid (line 17): pronounced and stressed /INvalid/. An invalid is someone who is permanently ill – or thinks s/he is.

woollen (line 31): Made from wool.

You can't help it (line 49): that is, 'it isn't your fault. You cannot do anything about it.'

Don't upset yourself (line 59): the same as 'Don't get upset'.

78

Glossary and Language Practice

fast asleep (line 66): a fixed expression meaning deeply asleep. Other examples: 'wide awake', 'blind drunk', 'stone deaf'.

a good night's sleep (line 66): the possessive form ('s/s') is found in a few fixed expressions, especially expressions to do with time. Other examples: a month's salary, three weeks' holiday.

he stuck his tongue out at her (line 71): this is the sort of thing that children do. It is very impolite, except when your doctor tells you to do it.

Hip! Hip! Hooray! (line 77): this is what you shout when you want to cheer or congratulate someone, for example, the winning football team.

forgotten all about me (line 94): 'all' emphasizes that he has completely forgotten about her. Other examples: 'Tell me all about yourself', 'I know all about you'.

She caught sight of the body on the floor (line 96): 'catch sight of' means that she suddenly noticed him.

shuffled (line 99): 'shuffling' describes the slow heavy walk of fat people wearing slippers.

LANGUAGE PRACTICE

A

Look at the story again to find answers to these questions:

1 What three things did Muff do wrong on this particular morning?
2 Had Mrs Muff always been an invalid?
3 What work did Mrs Muff give him to do that day? How did Muff feel about having to do those things?
4 Why was the best part of the day for Muff the time 'when he took his wife her cup of cocoa at night'?
5 What does the word 'it' refer to in line 49 ('You can't help it').

B

Fill in the missing words. Most of them are prepositions.

This morning was no different _____ all the other mornings. When they first met and fell _____ love she was strong and healthy, but soon _____ their marriage she became an invalid. The doctor didn't know what was wrong _____ her. Mrs Muff said that her problems were caused _____ 'nerves'. They had no children, so Muff had to look _____ her.

She didn't like his hat, so she told him to take it _____. Then she fell back _____ the pillows as if his hat had taken _____ all her strength.

The Penguin Book of Elementary Very Short Stories

Muff took _____ the hat and put it _____ his pocket.

C

All these irregular verbs are used in the story. Can you complete the table?

I take	I took	I have taken
become		
begin		
bend		
bring		
catch		
drink		
fall		
forget		
give		
hold		
keep		
leave		
mean		
read		
shake		
sing		
sit		
sleep		
spend		
stick		
throw		
upset		
wake up		

D

Discuss these questions with someone else who has also read the story

1. Do you think that Mrs Muff was really ill? Why had she become an invalid, do you think?
2. Did Muff really love his wife? What kind of man was he, do you think?
3. Without looking at the story, describe what Mrs Muff did after she realized that Muff was dead. From her actions, can you tell how she felt about her husband? Is there a difference between loving someone and needing someone?

Glossary and Language Practice

Black Mud

USEFUL VOCABULARY

Nouns

accent	goat	sunbathing
air	herd	sunlight
bathing costume	landscape	swimming
beach	Middle East	trunks
brochure	mud	tank
changing room	oil	tour
coach	peace	travel agent
couple	scene	trip
desert	soldier	tub

Verbs

book	hurt	sink
come off	miss = fail to reach	suit
float	look	wash off
guess	rush past	

Adjectives

ashamed of	crazy	peaceful
cheerful	crowded	rusty
cool	great = good	

Others

as well	side by side	What about . . .?
on leave	What a pity!	

GLOSSARY

the Sabbath (line 1): God created the world in six days, and He rested on the seventh day, which is called the Sabbath. For Jews the Sabbath is Saturday; for Christians it is Sunday.

travel agent's (line 3): the names of a number of shops or offices end in 's. Other examples: I went to the chemist's to get some medicine. Can you buy bread at the grocer's? No, only at the baker's.

The Penguin Book of Elementary Very Short Stories

brochure (line 7): originally a French word, it is pronounced /brouʃuə/.

sunbathing (line 10): from to 'sunbathe', it is pronounced /sʌnbeiðiŋ/.

float and *sink* (line 21): if you throw a piece of wood into the water, it will float; if you throw a stone, it will sink.

it didn't seem much of a tour (line 33): it did not seem to me to be a very good tour.

I guess (line 66): this use of 'guess' is American. English people would say 'suppose'.

It felt great (line 77): a popular way of saying that something is very good, or that you enjoyed it very much. 'How was the party?' 'Great! Really fantastic.'

Perhaps it won't come off! (line 85): perhaps you won't be able to wash it off later.

All good things must come to an end! (line 88): a common proverb.

LANGUAGE PRACTICE

A

Look at the story again to find answers to these questions:

1. Why did the writer decide to go on a coach tour?
2. What did the writer see (a) on the way to Jerusalem; (b) in the desert?
3. On first arriving at Ein Gedi, the writer felt sad? Why? Then the writer began to feel happier. What caused the change?
4. What did the writer mean by 'So have you. At least, I think you have!' (line 71).
5. What did the black man mean when he said: 'Perhaps it won't come off! Then you'll have a problem, won't you?' (line 85)?

B

Put in the missing words. We usually give you the first letters of the missing words. You can find all the expressions in the story.

1. I did _____ most visitors do: I went to a _____ _____'s to book a coach tour for the f_____ day.
2. I didn't want to go to a city. I preferred the f_____ air and peace of the _____side.
3. The br_____ had a _____ure of a beach sc_____ on the front.
4. I didn't want to sun_____ because I have fair sk_____ and I b_____ easily.

Glossary and Language Practice

5 Because the Dead Sea is so _____ of salt, you cannot s_____: you just _____ on your back and _____ in it.
6 The land _____ _____ Tel Aviv and Jerusalem is qu_____ pretty, except _____ the r_____y tanks by the roadside.
7 The boys we saw in the d_____ were looking _____ h_____s of goats.
8 The ch_____ room where we put _____ our bathing c_____ was in a large b_____ not far from the beach.
9 I thought the people on the beach were cr_____: they were taking mud _____ big t_____ and putting it over _____ _____'s bodies.
10 I tried to c_____ myself with mud, but I m_____ some places on my back because I _____n't r_____.

C

Fill in the missing words. In some cases, several different words will fit. Look at the text to see how well you have done.

'Well, if it's good _____ your skin, I guess _____ will be good for _____!' he said. He put _____ hands into the _____ and started to cover _____ in mud. We put mud on _____ other's backs and walked _____ into the water.

'Don't _____ to swim in it,' I said. 'It's _____ to put your face in the water. Just lie _____.'

There we were: two black bodies side _____ side under the hot _____ Eastern sun. All _____ us, people were enjoying _____. Some were standing in _____ water. Others were washing the mud _____. I felt safe under my _____ of mud: I was happy _____ my black body.

'All good things come to an _____!' he said suddenly.

D

Discuss these questions with someone else who has also read the story.

1 Is the 'I' of this story a man or a woman, do you think? Give reasons for your choice.
2 Starting with the scene on the beach at Ein Gedi, re-tell the story from the point of view of the black man. Would the world be a better place if we were all the same colour?

The Penguin Book of Elementary Very Short Stories

The Orinoco Treasure

USEFUL VOCABULARY

Nouns

accent	drawing	lipstick
accident	dream	nightclub
age	emerald	nurse
beard	estuary	plan
birth	handbag	profession
blouse	island	purpose
boat	jewel	report
circumstances	knowledge	skirt
customer	law	stockings
diamond	lawyer	treasure
document		

Verbs

add	join	promise
agree	keep away from	reply
cause	keep doing	shake
draw	match	stare
dream	nod	take no notice
drown	point to	throw
feel sorry for	pretend	wave
hear of	produce	whisper

Adjectives

boring	expensive	painted
cheap	friendly	shy
clever	local	silly
curious	lonely	successful
dead	painted	unbelievable
drunk	possible	

Others

as usual	Hello!	Never mind!
Cheers!	indeed	surely
Come on!	in fact	

Glossary and Language Practice

GLOSSARY

who have a lot of lipstick on (line 3): the same as 'who wear a lot of lipstick'.
twenty-eight or so (line 6): 'or so' means 'or a little bit more'.
Salute! ... Cheers! (line 20): pronounced /salU:te/. You lift your glass and say 'Cheers!' to wish the other person good health.
Yes, please join us (line 28): 'join us' means 'come and sit with us at our table'. If you wanted to sit with a group of people at a table, you would say 'Do you mind if I join you?'
dearest (line 51): a word of affection, like 'darling', but more often used by older people.
I was feeling lonely ... Eduardo was sitting alone (line 68): 'alone' means that nobody is with you; 'lonely' is the sad feeling you get because you are alone.
How are your studies going? (line 72): 'how is/are something/things going?' is a common expression used to ask if everything is well.
touching his nose (line 122): an Italian touches his nose to show that he knows the real truth, or that he shares the secret.
wishing she would kiss me (line 146): note the pattern after 'wish':
 I want you to do it, but I don't think you will – I wish you would do it.
 I wanted you to do it, but you didn't – I wish you had done it.
I was curious (line 156): I wanted to find out more about what had happened.
a cousin of mine (line 157): the same pattern as 'a friend of mine' 'a colleague of Bill's', etc.
Purpose of visit (line 164): that is 'Why did he come to Venezuela?'
Circumstances of death (line 166): that is, how, where and when did he die?

LANGUAGE PRACTICE

A

What is wrong with these statements?

1 Sybil and Eduardo were both Italians.
2 Miguel was in Rome on holiday.
3 Eduardo was a lecturer in law at the University in Rome.
4 Miguel first knew about the treasure when Sybil's father showed him the map.
5 Curiapo is an island at the mouth of the River Orinoco.
6 The treasure map was hundreds of years old.

The Penguin Book of Elementary Very Short Stories

7 Miguel borrowed a boat from his uncle to take Eduardo and Sybil to the island.
8 On his return to Venezuela, Miguel got a job on a local newspaper in Curiapo.
9 Miguel first heard about Eduardo's death from his cousin at the police station.
10 Miguel recognized Sybil in the newspaper photograph because of the jewels she was wearing.

B

Fill in the missing words. In some cases, several different words will fit. Look at the text to see how well you have done.

That night I _____ badly. I dreamed _____ red dresses and red lips and a woman's hand _____ an old man's grey head. For the next _____ weeks I kept _____ from the restaurant. But I _____ stop thinking about Sybil. Perhaps I was in _____ with her. _____ Friday evening I was feeling _____, so I went back _____. Eduardo was sitting alone. I _____ to go out again _____ Eduardo saw me. He shouted to me to _____ him. _____ my surprise, he was very friendly.

'Miguel, my friend, how _____ to see you again! _____ us have a drink and talk _____ law.'

C

Discuss these questions with someone else who has also read the story.

1 What do you learn from the story about the life and character of (a) Eduardo; (b) Miguel?
2 Eduardo and Sybil both wanted to find the treasure. Why did he need her? Why did she need him? Where did the map come from? What do you think finally happened?
3 Retell the story from Sybil's point of view. Do you think Miguel was right to call her a 'dangerous woman'?

Glossary and Language Practice

A Miracle on the Galata Bridge

USEFUL VOCABULARY

Nouns

angel	gallery	rest = remainder
art	horror	rubbish
boss	memory	saint
break = interval	miracle	sign
bridge	miss = young lady	silence
church	paint	spot = location
cloth	painting	square = place
corner	postscript	throne
damage	prayer	voice
entrance	problem	whitewash
expert		

Verbs

attack	cross	remove
be used to	forgive	reply
bother	murmur	rub
climb	pack	turn into
cover up	point	wipe

Adjectives

blank	miserable	polite
comfortable	pale	serious
employed	patient	shocked
excellent	perfect	terrible
fresh	pink	

Others

as far as	God willing	Thank Heavens
Excuse me	hardly	underneath

GLOSSARY

before returning (line 5): the same as 'before she returned'.

The Penguin Book of Elementary Very Short Stories

How's it going? (line 7): a common expression to ask about somebody's work, studies, life, etc.

whitewash (line 14): a mixture of chalk and water. It washes off quite easily.

The pink (line 15): that is, the colour pink.

Thank Heavens! (line 22): the same as Thank goodness! or Thank God!

Selim made a face (line 41): you 'make a face' to show that you don't like something.

She could hardly wait to ... (line 65): the expression means that she was very impatient to finish the job.

What do you do? (line 108): this is the question you ask when you want to know what job somebody has.

You will do very well (line 121): that is, you will be very successful.

in mid-sentence (line 130): in the middle of the sentence.

not believing her own eyes (line 141): she could not believe what she saw.

Postscript (line 147): something added at the end of a piece of writing. If you want to add something to a letter, put PS (for postscript), and then write the extra piece.

LANGUAGE PRACTICE

A

Look at the story again to find answers to these questions:

1. Who and what was Leyla referring to when she said (line 18) 'we have to be very careful'?
2. How did Selim feel about his work? Why?
3. What is 'the spot' (line 70)?
4. In her conversation with the young man on the bridge, several things surprised Leyla. What were they?
5. What was the 'something else' (line 144) that made Leyla so happy?

B

Fill in the missing words. In some cases, several different words will fit. Look at the text to see how well you have done.

Leyla went back _____ her painting on the _____ of the north gallery. _____ the days turned _____ weeks, more and _____ of the painting could _____ seen. Meral *hanim* was right: _____ was a picture _____ the throne of God with His angels _____ round. And Selim *bey* was right:

88

Glossary and Language Practice

they were _____ serious, they did not _____ happy, even _____ they were happy inside. The painting was _____ finished now, _____ for one small corner. She could _____ wait to finish the picture. She _____ up a fresh cloth and _____ the whitewash.

Too late! Leyla, who _____ always been so careful, rubbed _____ hard, and rubbed _____ the whitewash and the paint _____. She had rubbed _____ the angel's face!

C

Discuss these questions with someone else who has also read the story.

1 What do you learn from the story about Leyla's life and character?
2 It costs a lot of money to restore the paintings in Ayasofya. Museums and art galleries cost a lot of money. Is it money well spent? What do you like and/or dislike about museums?